Into the Wild Blue Yonder

NUMBER THIRTEEN
Centennial of Flight Series

Roger D. Launius, General Editor

INTO THE WILD BLUE YONDER

My Life in the Air Force

Allan T. Stein

TEXAS A&M UNIVERSITY PRESS   COLLEGE STATION

LIBRARY OF CONGRESS CATALOGING-IN-PUBLICATION DATA

Stein, Allan T., 1924–
    Into the wild blue yonder : my life in the Air Force / Allan T. Stein.—1st ed.
        p. cm.—(Centennial of flight series : no. 13)
    Includes index.
    ISBN 1-58544-386-7 (cloth : alk. paper)
    1. Stein, Allan T., 1924– 2. Bomber pilots—United States—Biography.
3. Air pilots, Military—United States—Biography. 4. United States. Air Force—
Officers—Biography. I. Title. II. Series.
UG626.2S738.A3   2005
358.4'0092—dc22   2004012922

To the men who flew for the U.S. Air Force
and especially those who were in the Strategic
Air Command, who stood ready to fight a nuclear
war with fifteen minutes notice, in the defense
of this country.

To SSgt. Raphael Sedlow, a twenty-
year-old waist gunner from Detroit,
Michigan, who gave his life for his
country during a horrible war so we can
live in peace.

To my loving wife, Eva, my partner and
companion for more than fifty-nine years
who, as an air force wife, kept the
home fires burning while I was wandering
around the world.

Contents

Preface

This is not the story of a great war hero. I did not win the Medal of Honor or even make headline news. The real heroes were those who were wounded or killed in the line of duty. This is instead the story of an ordinary air force pilot who, like thousands of others, loved his job and serving his country. The excitement of being a small part of the history of the U.S. Air Force makes me very proud.

My uncle was a pilot in World War I. It was because of his influence I decided on a career as an air force pilot. Serving one's country as a military officer is a very rewarding experience. I look back at my life in the air force with great pride, a feeling of accomplishment, and thankfulness that I was given an opportunity to serve.

As a young officer I tried to follow my superior officer's orders to the best of my ability and later, when I was in command, I expected the same of my subordinates. I always admired my commanders whose operating code was "follow me." Later when I was in command, I tried to copy that code.

I am writing this to relate some of my experiences and to share them with anyone who wonders what an air officer's life was like during the forties, fifties, and sixties when our country was in three conflicts and the Cold War. My experiences are not much different from any other air force pilot during the same period.

Some of my experiences during World War II have been difficult to relive as with most men who faced combat during that war. Not all of them were bad, however; some were very rewarding. I have added a few humorous stories to show the importance of a sense of humor even in dire circumstances.

World War II took place more than fifty-eight years ago and sometimes memories fail, but the dates of the missions flown were taken from logs maintained by the members of our B-24 crew. Since World War II our crew has had many reunions. Ask any military veteran and he will tell you that the reunions with his old military associates are some of the most enjoyable times of his retired life. During those reunions different crew members have brought up incidents that I had completely forgotten.

Through research at the Air Force Historical Research Agency at the Air University Library, Maxwell Air Force Base, Montgomery, Alabama, our World War II flight engineer located several reports about actual missions we flew while we were stationed at Clark Air Base on the island of Luzon in the Philippines. He also located a detailed description of a disastrous mission when one of our B-24s attacked an escorted convoy. This mission is covered in the text of this book.

I have related some historical events from my own personal experience. I feel everyone owes it to future generations to pass along what he has learned from his life. Too often this knowledge dies with the passing of generations. Events in history fly by so fast that it is important to keep a record of one's experience to pass on to the future.

This country was born in conflict and struggle. The early settlers who came here had to fight for their very lives to keep a foothold in those early days. They fought starvation, disease, and the unfriendly Indians along with the British and French. Each generation has had its own battles to fight. We have fought wars against Spain, Mexico, and even each other in the bloodiest of all the wars, the so-called Civil War. No war is civil. We were still fighting to keep this land just a little more than one hundred years ago.

My wife has a diary written by her great-grandfather, the Reverend L. B. Deaton, telling of his experiences during the Civil War. In it he expresses his political views as to what started the war, the effect it had on his own family, and the grief he suffered when his son was killed at Fort Donelson while serving in the Union army. Because he wrote the book, we have a clear picture of what happened to him and his family and what their lives were like at their time in history. It has inspired me to write this book—to reflect what life has been like during my time in history.

In the twentieth century we fought in two world wars against Germany, one war against Japan, and two against the Communists in Korea and in Vietnam. Today, we continue to put down petty dictators throughout the world as we are doing against Iraq.

Freedom is not cheap and is paid for by the life blood of those men and women who are willing to fight for it and sometimes it is necessary to fight for what we believe in. In that case I hope those young men and women who come after me will do so willingly and bravely.

The quality of the photographs taken during World War II are not only more than fifty years old, but they went through a typhoon while I was still in the Pacific. Some were not processed until I got back to the States.

The specifications listed with the pictures from the Air Force Museum are from the requirements the government specified when the plane was ordered. They do not reflect the way they were used by the air force. For example, the maximum gross weight of the B-24 was listed as 65,000 pounds. We routinely weighed 75,000 pounds on takeoff for a combat mission.

The actual fighting in World War II, as in most wars, was done by young people in their late teens and early twenties. They were young and strong and could stand the stresses and conditions of combat much better than older men. World War II was actually fought by civilians in military uniforms. Young men volunteered or were drafted right out of high school and off college campuses, given minimum training, and sent into combat. Leadership and experience were sorely lacking. People were promoted into positions they were completely unqualified to handle. These young men had to rely on inexperienced leaders who were trying to do the best they could.

During World War II, I was not a very religious person, even with the old saying that "there are no atheists in fox holes." At the time I based my survival on luck, chance, the enemy's poor marksmanship, and my rabbit's foot. Now that I am older, I look back at my military life and civilian life after I retired and realize someone has been watching over me. God has been with me.

Into the Wild Blue Yonder

chapter 1

Realizing the Dream

I CANNOT REMEMBER A TIME when I did not dream of being a military pilot. To explain my desire for a military career, I must go into my background as a young boy. While my father, Allan T. Stein Sr., was in Texas trying to recover from the Great Depression, my mother and I lived with my widowed grandmother, Martha Jack Anderson, in Rock Springs, Wyoming.

My uncle, Lt. Robert M. Anderson, had been a pilot in the 50th Aero Squadron of the American Expeditionary Forces (AEF) in France in 1918. He received a citation from General Pershing "for distinguished and exceptional gallantry at Buzancy, France on 3 November 1918." He also received the Silver Star when he and his Observer, Lt. Woodville Rogers, found the 308th Battalion (The Lost Battalion) of the 77th Infantry Division, which had been surrounded by the Germans and were sorely in need of food, ammunition, and medical supplies. When they were finally found, they were relieved by the Air Service who dropped supplies to them and were eventually rescued by the infantry.

Uncle Robert was like a father to me while my father was away. He talked to me about flying and how he had wanted a military career, but was forced to leave the Air Service after the war because his father, John M. Anderson, had died before the war and left a sheep ranch and some real estate that his mother was trying to hold together during the war. She needed his help.

After World War I Uncle Robert still had flying in his blood. He and another former member of the Air Service tried to start an air service flying from Rock Springs to Yellowstone Park. It did not work out because they could not get a suitable aircraft and people were afraid to fly. I spent a lot of time with Uncle Robert and he had such an impact on me that a record of my life without mentioning him would be incomplete.

My first recollection of his flying was around 1929 when I was just five years old. One of his friends from the Air Service's 50th Aero Squadron came through Rock Springs barnstorming with a World War I DH4

Lt. Robert M. Anderson, pilot, 50th Aero Squadron, AEF, World War I.

aircraft. He asked my uncle if he wanted to fly and, of course, Uncle Robert took him up on it. They had the whole town of Rock Springs staring spellbound at the sky as they performed aerobatic stunts. Everyone was convinced they were going to kill themselves. I do not think too many of the people in Rock Springs had ever seen an airplane at that time.

When Rock Springs decided it was time to build an airport, they asked Uncle Robert to lay it out since he was the only "authority" handy. I would ride my bike out to watch the few planes that landed there. Around 1933 I remember seeing a Martin B-10 bomber, "the air power wonder of its day." The army was displaying its new aircraft to the public by showing it around the country. It received a great deal of publicity in the Rock Springs newspaper. I rode my bicycle out to the airport and I got close enough to write my name on the tail. The B-10 was the most exciting thing I had ever seen. These memories and Uncle Robert's stories so intrigued me that I knew that I wanted to be a military pilot when I grew up.

In 1933, when I was nine years old, we moved to Houston, but every summer, my mother and I would go back to Wyoming to avoid the hot weather. I spent a lot of time on the family sheep ranch with Uncle Robert. Many of our conversations were "hanger flying."

The Anderson Ranch was about ninety miles north of Rock Springs and was about ten miles northwest of the old ghost town of South Pass. I must say here that Grandfather Anderson also had saloons in Rock Springs in the old days and at one time, Butch Cassidy was captured in one of them. There are many old stories handed down in the family about those early days in Wyoming, but that is another story.

Grandfather Anderson had sheep herds in the Wind River Mountains tended by Mexican nationals who lived in covered wagons. In the summer the herds were on the meadows in the mountains and in the winter they were moved to southern Wyoming.

It was a very remote area. My mother used to say that if we were ever invaded, she would head for the sheep camp; no one would ever find her there. The distance from Rock Springs to the Wind River Range was such that it was a long drive in those days over inferior roads by truck, so Uncle Robert built a ranch house to store supplies. I do not know if Uncle Robert learned his scrounging skills in the Air Service, but he always made use of anything someone else threw away. The ranch house was nothing more than a one-room shack built out of lumber from an

Lieutenant Anderson with the DeHavilland DH-4.

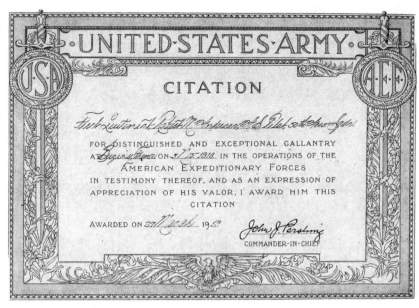

Citation signed by Gen. John J. Pershing.

old train depot. He may have been an excellent pilot, but he was not a very good carpenter. None of the windows or the door were plumb. It was not considered all that necessary. It had room for a bed, a stove, a table, and two benches. We did not need an ice box. The weather was cool enough to keep food from spoiling. We got fresh water from a spring by the cabin. Uncle Robert also built a two-hole outhouse made out of logs with a wool sack for a door and a Sears Roebuck catalog for "convenience." Uncle Robert and Aunt Ruth slept in the cabin, but my cousin, my mother, and I slept in a tent. We would spend our summers at the ranch.

There were no stores, so supplies had to be ordered from Sears Roebuck in Denver. One day some of the sheep ranchers were sitting around talking and one said, "You can get anything from Sears Roebuck." Another rancher said, "Oh yeah, let me see you get a sheep herder." A bet was made and they placed an order to Sears for a sheep herder. It was forgotten until one day about three weeks later, a fellow showed up to say he was a sheep herder and had been sent by Sears Roebuck. The Sears slogan at that time was "Sears Has Everything." Indeed they did.

I look back on it now and realize that it was not much of a place to live, but it was a great place for kids to grow up. The only time I remember getting into trouble was when my cousin and I put a cat in the storage box where the meat was stored. Boy, did we catch hell over that!

When I was seven years old, my father sent me five dollars to buy a 22-caliber rifle. The population of Wyoming was so sparse that there would not be another human being within miles of the ranch, especially in the 1930s. They'd tell me, "Don't shoot back toward the ranch." I could fire in any other direction and not have to worry about hitting anyone. While I was out hunting "big game," I shot a rabbit. I wanted to keep it and stuff it. I found the project rather distasteful after a few days and gave it up. I did keep the rabbit's foot however and I carried that rabbit's foot around with me all through World War II. It brought me luck.

One time the sheep herders ran across an antelope fawn that kept wondering back into the sheep camp. They had to protect it from the sheep dogs. The doe did not seem to be around, so they put it in the back of a truck and brought it to the ranch for my cousins and me to look after. We filled an empty beer bottle with canned milk and water, and put a nipple on it and fed him. He spent the entire summer with us. By the fall when it was time for us to go back to town to start to school, the fawn was old enough to turn loose. I still remember the sound of his footsteps early in the morning when he would come in and get in bed with me. I would have to get up and feed him.

SPECIFICATIONS
Span: 70 ft. 6 in.
Length: 44 ft. 9 in.
Height: 15 ft. 5 in.
Weight: 14,700 lbs. loaded
Armament: 3 .30 cal. machine
 guns, 2,200 lbs. of bombs
Engines: Two Wright R-1820's
 of 775 hp ea.
Cost: $55,000

PERFORMANCE
Maximum speed: 215 mph
Cruising speed: 183 mph
Range: 1,370 miles
Service ceiling: 24,000 ft.

MARTIN B-10

The B-10, the first of the "modern-day" all-metal monoplane bombers to be produced in quantity, featured such innovations as internal bomb storage, retractable landing gear, a rotating gun turret, and enclosed cockpits. It was so advanced in design that it was 50 percent faster than its contemporary biplane bombers and as fast as most of the fighters. When the Air Corps ordered 121 B-10s in the 1933-36 period, it was the largest procurement of bomber aircraft since WW I. It also ordered 32 B-10 type bombers with Pratt and Whitney rather than Wright engines and designated these as B-12s.

General Henry H. "Hap" Arnold once called the B-10 the air power wonder of its day. In 1934 he led ten B-10s on a 7,360 mile flight from Washington, D.C. to Fairbanks, Alaska and back. Although Air Corps B-10s and B-12s were replaced by B-17s and B-18s in the late 1930s, China and the Netherlands flew export versions in combat against Japan.

Martin B-10 bomber, which featured internal bomb storage, retractable landing gear, a rotating gun turret, and enclosed cockpits.

Just before it was time to start to school in the fall, I went back to Rock Springs and got a haircut and a tub bath. Up in the mountains living in a tent, one does not have the luxury of a tub bath. There were some orphaned lambs that we brought back to town and kept in a pen in the backyard. It was my job to see to it that they were fed and watered. When I came home from school in the afternoons, they would come running to the fence to be fed. They stayed there until they were old enough to join the herd. They became pets and to this day, I cannot eat lamb.

In 1939, my father took my mother and me for a tour of San Antonio. We went to Randolph Army Air Field, which was then known as the "West Point of the Air." After seeing the cadets learning to fly, all my uncle's stories came back to me, and it reinforced my burning desire to have a military career.

I did not have a record of Uncle Robert's flying experiences in World War I until he was an old man in his nineties living with his daughter, Bobbie Jane, in Salt Lake City. All I had was my memory of our conversations when we were both much younger. My wife, Eva, and I drove from Houston to Salt Lake City for a visit. I am so thankful I had an opportunity to have a conversation with him like we had years ago about the family history and his World War I experiences. This time I recorded our conversation. This was the last time I saw this dear man before he died. I have letters he wrote to his mother and sister (my mother) about his training and experiences in France and also copies of his official army records. Many articles have been written about his service during World War I. He left me his Silver Star medal, his helmet, his barometer he obtained from the French, a photo album, and mementoes of his service.

I graduated from Lamar High School in Houston in June, 1941. I had my seventeenth birthday in August and went to Texas A&M University to major in aeronautical engineering. At that time, A&M was an all-male, full-time military school from which I would receive a commission as a second lieutenant in the coast artillery. Many of the officers who served in World War II came from A&M. There were 6,600 cadets there my freshman year and 10,000 my sophomore year. Because of World War II, many young men went to A&M for the military training and a chance for a commission.

Part of our coast artillery training was learning how to fire a cannon. We trained on a split trail 155-mm cannon, called a Long Tom. When we were preparing the gun to simulate firing, it was necessary to dig pits, one

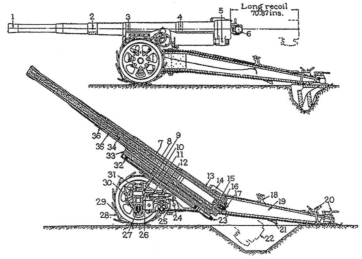

Plate 64. 155-mm Gun and Carriage (Side View and Section).

1. Muzzle bell
2. Clip hoop screw
3. Hoop screw
4. Jacket screw
5. Recoil lug
6. Breechblock
7. Hoop A
8. Recoil cylinder
9. Elevating rack
10. Cradle assembled
11. Traversing mechanism
12. Elevating mechanism
13. Jacket
14. Counterpoise cylinder
15. Breech mechanism
16. Breech ring
17. Firing mechanism
18. Traversing-bar lock
19. Trail
20. Spade clamping bolts
21. Limber stop
22. Short recoil
23. Piston-rod nut
24. Top carriage
25. Chassis (bottom carriage)
26. Traversing worm
27. Axle spring
28. Caterpillar band segment
29. Caterpillar band shoe
30. Brake rocker arm
31. Gun axle
32. Recoil piston
33. Cradle
34. Tube
35. Hoop B
36. Clip hoop

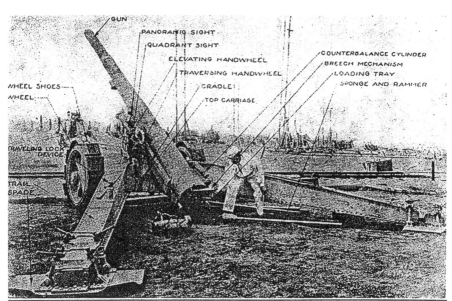

155-mm Gun in Firing Position.

A Long Tom, or a 155-mm cannon.

on each side, for two 500-pound spades, which supported the cannon, one attached to each of the trails. This was to keep the gun from rolling backward when it was fired. In addition it was also necessary to dig a six-foot recoil pit in the center. Two of us were given the job of picking up the 96-pound projectile, which sat on a 20-pound cradle, and lifting it up over our heads so the projectile could be rammed into the breech. I weighed 120 pounds and the other guy was as scrawny as I was. We could not even pick it up off the ground, much less lift it over our heads. We were trained by pre–World War II regular army sergeants who were considerably tougher then than they are now. The sergeant grabbed me by the arm and yanked me out of the recoil pit and gave me the job of closing the breech after the projectile and the powder bags were rammed home. The breech was so heavy, I could not move it. I can still hear him. "Stiff-arm it, goddamit. Stiff-arm it." I gave it all I had, but I still could not move it, so he yanked me away from that and gave me a job I could handle, putting the primer in the breech and pulling the lanyard.

There was no air force reserve at that time, but I felt certain I would be allowed to transfer to the army air corps when the time came. On December 7, 1941, "the date that will live in infamy," I guess I had done something one of the sophomores did not like, which did not take much. I was walking off demerits and guarding a tree with my rifle when someone yelled out the dorm window and said the Japanese had just bombed Pearl Harbor. I did not even know where Pearl Harbor was, but that day changed a lot of lives, including mine. It also sped up my plans for a military career by about four years. I was seventeen years old by three months and away from home for the first time.

When we entered Texas A&M, we were issued rifles. After the war broke out, we had reveille thirty minutes earlier. Schedules were changed to year-round semesters enabling us to graduate earlier. We spent the extra time doing rifle calisthenics. This increased our feelings that we were about to be called to active duty at any time. The main topic of conversation among the students for the next several months was about when we would be called to active duty. Rumors flew that should have been killed by the commandant of cadets. He should have explained to the first- and second-year cadets that we were too young and the army did not want us, that we should concentrate on our education because if the war lasted long enough we would be called up. With the hazing, taking aeronautical engineering, and the war, it was difficult to concentrate on anything.

I stayed in school taking a full course through the summer of 1942. In the fall we were told that if we joined the Coast Artillery Enlisted Reserve, we could remain in school, so on December 12, 1942, I enlisted. I was so young, I had to have my parent's permission. Ironically all voluntary enlistments were stopped by executive order on December 13, 1942. This was when I first learned never to trust a recruiting sergeant.

Less than two months later, my roommate, Bill Banister, and I checked the mail after breakfast. Bill received a letter from his father, Col. John Banister, who was deputy director of the Selective Service for the State of Texas in Austin. In the letter were orders calling Bill and me to active duty in the coast artillery, reporting to Camp Rosecrans, California. Colonel Banister also included everything Bill and I needed to transfer to the air corps and a note saying he could hold up the orders for three or four days and for Bill and me to go to Houston as soon as possible and transfer into the air corps. After my experiences with the 155-mm Long Tom, I knew there had to be something better. We left immediately and that evening we were in the air corps with an appointment to flight training. After we were sworn in, the lieutenant in charge asked us when we would like to go on active duty. I said I would like to go as soon as possible. Bill said he would like another semester in school. Knowing how the army does things, Bill left in a few weeks and I got the extra semester. I shall be forever grateful to Colonel Banister, for if he had not intervened, I might have wound up in the infantry or artillery as many of my classmates did.

When I enlisted, I had no thoughts of saving the world for freedom and democracy. I, like so many other young men, was caught up in a wave of patriotism and peer pressure. I was only seventeen years old by three months when Pearl Harbor was attacked and had no idea what war was all about.

On April 1, 1943, when I was in my junior year, I was ordered to active duty in the army air forces, reporting to the Houston army recruiting office. There was a large group of us, reporting at the same time. We were marched from the recruiting office at Market Square in downtown Houston to the Southern Pacific Railroad Station where we boarded a troop train headed for Sheppard Army Air Field, Wichita Falls, Texas, for basic training.

Before I left home my father gave me $5.00 to tide me over until I received my first pay. Our train stopped in Dallas and we were all herded into a dining room for breakfast. I was shocked when the army paid the check. I was naive enough to think that if they kept this up, surely the army would go broke.

Our group was joined by a group from the Universities of Montana and Idaho. Basic training lasted only about two weeks. We received physical examinations, were issued uniforms, given some close order drill, and then put back on a train. They did not tell us where we were going. Our destination was "top secret," but we headed south stopping at, of all places, Texas A&M at College Station.

The recruiting of prospective aviation cadets had exceeded the construction of training facilities and aircraft. The surplus of the applicants were sent to colleges all over the United States, known as College Training Detachments (CTD). We were called "aviation students."

While waiting for openings in flight training, we were sent back to college. I received another semester before being transferred. While at CTD, I received ten hours of introductory flight time in an Interstate Cub. We received very little instruction on the aircraft flight controls. It was not until I got to primary flight training that I was told that the rudder pedals were used for directional control of the airplane. I thought they were just some place to rest your feet.

We received lots of physical training while we were there. Our instructor was an "old man" about thirty-five to forty years old. On the first day he gave us about an hour of continuous calisthenics and he kept right up with us. When we finished the calisthenics, he said there would be a two-mile road run. We all laughed and nudged each other. This is where we were going to show the "old man" up. He led the group and disappeared ahead of us. When we finished, we were huffing and puffing and he was sitting in the shade of a tree waiting for us. He had earned our respect from that time on.

chapter 2
Pilot Training

IN AUGUST of 1943, we were sent to the San Antonio Aviation Cadet Classification Center (SAACCC), where we were given various tests to determine the type of training we were to receive. The tests were very comprehensive and took two to three days. Some of the cadets went to navigator training and some to bombardier training. I was relieved to be classified for pilot training, so on my nineteenth birthday, August 29, 1943, I entered pre-flight training at the San Antonio Aviation Cadet Center (SAACC), which is now Lackland Air Force Base. Pre-flight lasted for two months, during which time we received basic ground school training that consisted of aircraft identification, both friendly and enemy, map reading, navigation, and Morse code. We were required to be able to receive fifteen words per minute to complete pre-flight training.

There was also a great deal of physical training. We got "open post" for six to eight hours three times while we were there and were given passes to go into San Antonio. We were nineteen-year-old kids away from home for the first time, so we were anxious to take full advantage of the time off.

We went down to the famous River Walk where there was a patio in front of a restaurant overlooking the San Antonio River. We tried to drink as much beer as we could in the little time we had. It was only ten cents a bottle. Our entertainment was watching some of the beer-filled cadets in canoes riding down the river and falling in.

When we got back to the base, Corporal John, our physical training instructor, would say, "We are now going to work off all the beer you guys drank in town." I think he had a mission to try to kill us. We were thrilled when he left to go to officers' candidate school. We were shocked when we got to advanced flight training to find that our physical training instructor was Lieutenant John, again, and he had not mellowed one bit. I am reminded of those days in San Antonio every time I go back there and see the new young airmen enjoying their first open post.

While at SAACC, every Saturday morning we had an inspection. Afterwards, we were issued fresh class "C" uniforms, which had to be worn to class for the next week. The class "C" uniform was nothing more than government issue (GI) khaki pants, cut off at the knees for summer wear in the hot Texas climate, and regular GI shirts with the sleeves cut off at the elbow.

One day while we were waiting in line to get a fresh uniform, the supply sergeant pulled me out of line and told me to issue the uniforms. The cadets were in excellent physical condition and most of the sizes were 28–32. The uniforms to be issued were in a big stack with the sizes marked on the inside waistband and collar. While going through the stack looking for sizes as they were called out, I found a pair of size 48 pants. I set them aside waiting for the right person to come through. My good friend, Jim Terrell from Pocatello, Idaho, was the right person. I tossed him the size 48 pants thinking we would have a good laugh, and I would give him the right size, but instead of looking at them, he just took the pants and left. After all the uniforms were issued and we were back in the barracks, the public address system sounded saying, "Class 44-E, fall out in the company street in class 'C' uniforms in five minutes." We all put on our uniforms and started out the door. When Jim put on the size 48 pants, he completely panicked, because things too horrible to mention happened if you missed a formation. We were all lined up in formation when Jim came out of the barracks. It was just like a Max Synnot comedy. There was a street full of people all in hysterics. We had a nasty little second lieutenant in charge. He put his head on his forearm up against a light pole. His shoulders were shaking; we never knew if he was laughing or crying. The leg of those pants hit Jim at mid-calf and wrapped around him twice. There was room in the seat for Jim and a couple of watermelons. After order was restored, we did what was planned and Jim went back to supply to exchange the pants, but they told him to come back the next Saturday; there would be no exchanges. In pre-flight we had to double-time every place we went. Jim would run three steps and those pants would only move two. People came from all over the base to see Jim in those pants. I had a big problem from then on. I had to be ahead of Jim in that line on Saturday morning.

Even with all this, to his credit, we were good friends. We went completely through pilot training and graduated together. After graduation I went one way and he went another, but one day I was in a chow line in New Guinea, and I felt a hot breath on my neck and heard someone say, "you sonofabitch." I turned around to find Jim. We had some good laughs, ate together, and I never saw him again. I hope he survived the war.

Primary Flight Training

In November, I was sent to primary flight training at Gibbs AAFB, a World War II temporary base, at Fort Stockton, Texas. When the train arrived, we were ordered off, but there was no station or town. At first glance we figured someone had made a mistake. What a dismal sight. There was nothing but mesquite brush, flat land, and mesas. Finally a bus came to pick us up. To say we were excited is an understatement. This is the place that we were finally going to learn to fly. However, as our bus was pulling onto the base, we followed a flat bed truck that was carrying the remains of a training plane in which a cadet had just been killed. This was a very sobering sight. I do not think any of us were feeling too cocky after that.

We spent about four hours a day in ground school, and the remainder of the day on the flight line. Our training planes were Fairchild PT-19s, with two-place tandem seats and open cockpits. They had 175-hp Ranger engines with wooden propellers and fixed landing gear. The only means of communication between the cockpits was a rubber hose attached to the student's helmet, while the instructor spoke into a funnel at the other end. Crude, primitive, and did not work too well.

On November 22, I was flying with my instructor when we shot a landing. When we stopped, he got out and said, "You've got it; don't kill yourself." There I was at last, in the air all by myself. It was great until I realized that I had to get back on the ground in one piece. I had nine hours of instruction time when I soloed. The instructors were civilians who were too old for military service. They all had a lot of flying time and were very well qualified.

One day while I was waiting to fly with my instructor, I was sitting on a bench watching other cadets shooting landings. I happened to look up and saw someone falling through the sky. In a few seconds a parachute opened up and he landed at the edge of the field. A Jeep was sent to pick him up. It seems that the instructor was demonstrating a slow roll and the cadet had neglected to fasten his seat belt and while the plane was upside down, he fell out. For the rest of the time in primary flying school, he was used as a bad example. *Fasten your seat belt so you will not fall out of the airplane, especially if you are flying solo.*

Had most of the students soloed, the congestion at Gibbs would have been too great for safety. An alternate field, called Dyke Field, had been built a few miles away from Gibbs for students to practice landings. In the center of the field there was a control tower where the instructors could watch their students. It was only two stories high and there was no glass in the windows. Beside it was an outhouse. I flew over to Dyke Field with my instructor and when we landed, there was a crosswind. My instructor, Jim Weaver from Rock Springs, Texas, demonstrated how to make a crosswind landing by dropping the wing into the wind and using the opposite rudder to keep the plane going straight. After we landed he got out and told me to practice landings. On my first landing, I did everything perfectly—except in reverse. I added power to make a "missed approach" and just missed the control tower. At this point I was just hanging on. On my next landing, I realized the errors of the last landing and made a good landing. As I taxied by the control tower, my instructor leaned out the window and yelled, "Take it around again and this time see if you can't hit the shit-house."

After I made my last landing and parked the plane, people were still laughing. I didn't know what was so funny until they told me what happened. It seems that when I just missed the tower, I also just missed the outhouse. One of the cadets was in the outhouse at the time. When I flew over, they said he dove out the door with his pants down around his ankles.

When Christmas came around my parents came out to spend Christmas with me. I had broken one of the rules, something about doing a spin too close to the ground. I cannot remember exactly. At any rate, on Christmas Eve I was walking off demerits with a "1903" Springfield rifle. It was snowing and I was freezing. The TAC Officer in charge came out finally and said, "Peace on Earth, you guys get the hell out of here." It was Christmas Eve and I guess he did not want to be on duty either.

Basic Flight Training

In January, 1944, I completed primary flight training and was transferred to Goodfellow Army Air Field, San Angelo, Texas, for basic flight training. We trained in Vultee BT-13s. This plane also had tandem seats, but with a sliding canopy and an electronic intercom system. It had a fixed landing gear and a 450-hp Pratt Whitney radial engine with a two-speed metal propeller.

After soloing, we were introduced to night flying and night landings, which included a night solo flight. We were also introduced to instruments, formation flying, cross-country, and aerobatics. Many of the instructors were service pilots who had been civilian pilots of military age with a minimum amount of flying time. They were given direct commissions as second lieutenants and service pilot ratings, meaning they did not go through the regular cadet program. The remainder of the instructors were recent graduates from pilot training who tried to cover their lack of experience with a tough attitude. The "wash-out," or elimination rate, was quite high. I believed it was caused by poor instructors. At any rate, we were very concerned about being able to qualify and worried about "washing out."

Basic was rather uneventful. The food was excellent. There was a $50-per-month allowance for each cadet and the money went directly to the cadet mess. Periodically we would receive a package of cigarettes along with our meal. There was little entertainment on the base and I do not remember ever going into San Angelo. We were either flying, in ground school, in physical training, or in bed. There was not too much time off.

Most of the training bases were hastily constructed in small towns away from large populated areas. The buildings were built of wood and were meant to last only seven years. There was a headquarters building, barracks for the cadets, and a small post exchange where we could buy such basic needs as soap, toothpaste, shaving cream, and razor blades, not that many of us needed them. There was also a chapel and a theater. Sparse by today's standards, but it met the needs of our country's efforts in trying to mobilize in a hurry. Our quarters were open bay barracks. We were a little crowded; however, this problem solved itself with the elimination rate of cadets washing out. The heating system did not work too well and it became quite cold at night.

One day I was out on a solo cross-country flight to Hobbs, Texas, which was only about eighty miles from San Angelo. While I was looking for checkpoints on the map, flying the airplane, and trying not to get lost, a P-47 fighter pulled along side of me. I looked over to see what it was and its canopy was open and there was long hair blowing in the wind. It was a girl! She waved to me, gave it power, and disappeared. Women pilots were rare in those days. She was most likely a WASP ferry pilot.

The training program was at the mercy of the weather. In pre-flight there was no flying so the weather was not a factor. The weather at Fort Stockton was excellent and no flying days were lost, so we were able to get some time off and go into the town of Fort Stockton two times. In basic and advanced, flying days were lost to weather. These days were made up on weekends. As a result we never got to go into San Angelo or Lubbock.

We had one tragedy while at Goodfellow. One of our group, Aviation Cadet Wesley Cordes, was killed in a mid-air collision.

Multi-Engine Advanced Training

I completed basic flight training in March, 1944, and was designated for multi-engine training. Others were sent to single-engine fighter training. My next stop was Lubbock Army Air Field for advanced training. Our training aircraft were AT-17s, sometimes called UC-78s. It was a small, twin-engine plane with side-by-side controls, capable of carrying three passengers. It had retractable landing gear, variable pitch propellers, and two 245-hp radial Jacobs engines. The course consisted primarily of the effect of multi-engine flying. We also received instruction in formation, cross-country flights, and a great amount of instrument flying.

One night after landing, I came to the end of the runway. The tower had said, "Turn left after landing." Unfortunately, it was pitch black and I got confused and turned right. All of a sudden I began to go down and before I knew it, I was in a dry lake bed. I turned the plane around and tried to taxi back out. The plane did not have enough power to make it up the hill. I tried another spot with the same result. I kept moving around the lake bed until I finally found a spot low enough that I could get out. Those who say "nothing can stop the Army Air Corps" have not tried to taxi out of a dry lake bed.

The instructors were unqualified, or at best, had minimum qualifications. My instructor graduated in the class ahead of me and had about fifty hours more flying time than I did. He was at a complete loss on instrument flying. It was a lot like the "dumb leading the blind." I feel really fortunate that I was able to satisfactorily complete my final check-ride before graduation. This is not a reflection on the men. It was just the way things were during World War II. Because the United States had to mobilize in such a hurry, they had to make use of their trained pilots in combat zones. They were doing the best they could with what they had.

We tore up a lot of aircraft due to the lack of quality in the training we were getting. At a pre-takeoff briefing one morning, the flight commander congratulated us for not tearing up an airplane in three days. One day had been a Sunday and the other two days, the weather was so bad we could not fly.

Our instructors were always telling us how lucky we were to be able to go into combat while they were "stuck there not seeing any action." One day the flight commander asked for volunteers for combat and one of the instructors got up and said, "I'll go." I never saw so many people who all had to go to the bathroom at the same time. The rest of the instructors disappeared. That was the end of comments about wanting to go to combat.

Graduation day was May 23, 1944. I was nineteen years old. Up to this point I never gave much thought as to why I was being trained to be a multi-engine pilot. It was all a big adventure where we were caught up in the excitement of learning to fly an airplane. During my complete training, I received 216 hours of flying time, hardly enough to be considered a competent pilot ready for combat. I did not know what it would be like in combat, but felt I had not received sufficient training. The army air forces was in desperate need of pilots. As an illustration, several graduates were called and told that they were to be picked up that night and flown to various combat zones. They were going directly from pilot training into combat with a little more than two hundred hours flying time. The reason for the training had suddenly become very clear.

Prior to the attack on Pearl Harbor, the United States was not prepared for global conflict. President Roosevelt was concerned about Britain's ability to build a war machine qualified to compete with Germany in Europe. He began putting the industry of the United States on a wartime basis. He required an increase in aircraft production to fifty thousand planes per year. Prior to that, the U.S. Army Air Forces had fewer than seven hundred bombers of all types and less than half were combat ready.

There was a continuing demand for pilots and bomber crews. Many were lost in the high altitude daylight bombing raids over military and industrial targets in Europe. The German Luftwaffe was very efficient, and destroyed a lot of our bombers. The need for pilots was so great that the U.S. pilot training period was reduced by one month.

We were given money to buy our officer's uniforms because, as cadets, we were only paid enough barely to get by. We put on our new uniforms for the first time for our graduation ceremony. After the ceremony was over, we went to the cadet mess for lunch where we had always eaten. We were turned away because we were now officers and were not allowed to eat there. We went to the Officers' Club where we felt out of place and everyone looked at the brand new second lieutenants as if we had just stolen the front door of the club.

Graduation day, D Flight, Class 44E, Lubbock Army Air Field, May 23, 1944. Author appears in back row, third from left.

I did not get an assignment after graduation, but was given a two-week leave and told to report back to Lubbock Army Air Field for assignment. So I went home to Houston for the first time since that day I first boarded the train for Sheppard Field in April, 1943.

I was now a "professional pilot." I had the wings to prove it. I was at once proud and relieved that I had made the grade, and apprehensive about the future because I knew I was headed for combat. I had no idea where I would go . . . to Europe? to the Pacific? or what kind of plane I would be flying.

While I was in Houston on leave, June 6, 1944, D-Day occurred. The whole nation's attention was focused on the news and what was happening in Europe. People were elated that the long-expected invasion had come at last. At the same time, they were also thinking of the thousands of American boys taking part in it. It was a time of great expectation and anxiety for the families of the young men involved. We were confident of victory over the Nazis, but also knew that many American lives would be sacrificed. It was a time unique in American history and I knew that I would soon become a part of it.

After I reported back to Lubbock Army Air Field for an assignment, there was no place to stay. Rooms at the Officer's Quarters were full, but cots were set up in an empty building where we stayed until we moved on.

chapter 3

Combat Crew Training

UPON RETURNING TO LUBBOCK Army Air Field, I received
orders to Lincoln Army Air Field, a World War II temporary base, at Lincoln, Nebraska, where I received an assignment as a copilot on a B-24 crew.
The crew roster was as follows:

Lt. William A. Canevari, pilot, 22, California
Lt. Allan T. Stein, copilot, 20, Texas
Lt. William F. Clark, navigator, 22, Rhode Island
Lt. Eugene R. Burns, bombardier, 21, California
Cpl. Paul M. Stanfield, flight engineer, 21, Virginia
Cpl. Emery J. Melancon, radio operator, 20, Louisiana
Cpl. Edward P. Dowling, waist gunner, 20, Pennsylvania
Cpl. Raphael Sedlow, waist gunner, 20, Michigan
Sgt. William H. Lee, nose gunner, 21, Texas
Pfc. William Rowe, tail gunner, North Carolina

These ages are as of 1944. I had my twenty-first birthday while I was in the
Pacific. Most of the rest of the crew had just graduated from high school
before entering the service. The entire crew with the exception of the pilot
had just completed their technical training. The pilot graduated from flight
training the class before me. While I was completing advanced pilot training
and on leave, he went to B-24 Transition, where he received some training in
the aircraft. With the experience of the crew members, by today's standards,
it was a disaster waiting to happen and was a main factor in the high casualty rate among bomber crews. There again, the United States was doing the
best it could with what it had. There just was not time for more training. In
looking back now, it was a miracle that anyone survived. Not all of us did.

While I was at Lincoln, Bill Banister, my Texas A&M roommate, showed
up. He had just graduated from pilot training also and was there getting
his crew assignment. He went from there to Casper, Wyoming, for combat crew training. We enjoyed a good reunion for a few days.

The crew. Standing, left to right: Lts. Bob Burns, Bill Clark, Al Stein, and Bill Canevari. Kneeling, left to right: Bill Rowe, Bill Lee, Raphael Sedlow, Pat Dowling, Red Melancon, and Paul Stanfield.

Our crew was transferred to Gowen Army Air Field, another World War II temporary base in Boise, Idaho, where I was born. There, we received combat crew training.

I will never forget my first impression of a B-24. By comparison with the training planes I had been flying, it was gigantic. The wing span was 110 feet and it had four 1,200–horse power engines. I could not see how anything that big could fly. In comparing it with today's bombers, it was quite small. The aircraft we were to train in were completely equipped for combat.

The training was based on the type of combat operations in the European Theater of Operations (ETO), which was primarily high altitude formation. The training was very realistic. We flew in a combat box formation with six B-24s in the lead flight. There were three other flights of six each: a high flight to the right and above the lead flight, a low flight to the left of the lead flight, and one to the rear directly behind the lead flight and below the left flight for a total of twenty-four planes. We would be joined by combat boxes from Casper Army Air Field, Wyoming, and Pocatello Army Air Field, Idaho, making a 72-plane formation. We would make simulated bomb runs on Salt Lake City while we were being attacked by fighters from Wendover Army Air Field, Utah. We would be flying at 25,000 to 30,000 feet, which must have been a very impressive sight from the ground.

We also practiced navigation, gunnery, and dropping 100-pound sand-filled practice bombs. We completed training on September 12, 1944, and were given ten-day leaves before reporting to Topeka Army Air Field, Kansas, where we were to process for the ETO. I was headed for combat with 156 hours in a B-24 with a total of 371 hours of flying time. That was not much training considering what we were going into.

When I went to Houston, Eva and I were married on September 16, 1944. After a two-day honeymoon in Galveston, I headed for Topeka, Kansas, and took Eva with me. At Topeka the graduating class from Boise was met by those who had completed training at Casper, Wyoming, and Pocatello, Idaho. I was coming out of the club one day, when I heard a very familiar laugh. I turned to see Banister on the back of a truck. He was leaving the base for Europe. We yelled at each other and he said, "I'll see you after the war." He was sent to Italy and flew bomb runs over German industrial targets. He was shot down twice and the Yugoslav partisans helped him back to his base.

There were well more than one hundred combat crews there. We were placed on a troop train headed for Langley Army Air Field, Virginia, a port of embarkation. You can imagine how Eva must have felt, a young girl all alone, on her own in a strange town with me headed for combat in the ETO. She returned home alone. She was met at the train by her father who told her that her mother had just been diagnosed with advanced breast cancer. It was quite a blow. She had gotten an indoctrination as an air force wife early in life. We were no longer children. The days of innocence were over.

Low Altitude Bomb Training

We arrived at Langley Army Air Field around October 1, 1944, and our crew, plus eleven other crews from Boise, were pulled out of the group. We were to get additional training on a new bomb sight that was especially designed for low altitude bombing (LAB). The radar antenna was placed in the position of the ball turret, so we no longer had a ball turret gunner, also no protection from enemy fighters from below. Flying at low altitude, the ball turret was no longer needed.

We received an additional crew member, a radar operator, Cpl. Casimer Sypniewski. The tail gunner, Bill Rowe, was transferred to a crew ready to go overseas. I did not find out until long afterwards that the enlisted men on the crew tried to hide Bill so he would not have to go. The people in the personnel office said that they would court-martial all of the enlisted men if they did not produce him, so we lost Bill on the crew. The officers knew nothing about the enlisted men's efforts.

Most of the time at Langley was spent perfecting the use of the new bomb sight by glide bombing and skip bombing targets in a bomb range in the Atlantic Ocean. We flew four anti-submarine patrol missions in the Atlantic. We were told we would be in training at Langley for a couple of months, so Eva joined me.

We checked in at the Hampton Roads Hotel and Eva spent a few fruitless days looking for a place to live, but could find nothing available. Trying to find housing off base was difficult with all of the servicemen moving about with their families. We finally settled for a room with kitchen privileges in a house owned by a woman whose husband was away in the navy. She rented out rooms to make ends meet. We had a bedroom and were allowed to use the kitchen. We were thrilled to get it. Living in the same house was Bill Lee, our nose gunner, with his wife and baby. We were the only ones on the crew who were married. As newlyweds we really enjoyed our few weeks together.

Early in the morning of December 17, 1944, our flight engineer, Paul Stanfield, came by our room and told us we were leaving around noon for the west coast. The troop cars were to be attached to a regular civilian train. I had to leave with Paul, but told Eva to meet me at the train station at Hampton Roads and we could ride together as far as St. Louis. We thought she would be heading back home to Houston on the same train. I got her a ticket to Houston and when we arrived at the train station, she was sitting there on a foot locker that held everything we owned. We boarded the train and found seats in the civilian cars. I had to go back to the troop cars, and told her I would be back as soon as we had a roll call. When I had a chance to sit with her, I started for her car but found nothing but empty track. Our cars had been disconnected at Newport News. We had ridden together for seven miles! She was on her own again and I did not see her again for almost a year, when I returned from the Pacific after the war was over. We never had a chance to say good-bye. It was quite a shock for both of us.

The troop train stopped for a few minutes in Cheyenne, Wyoming, and I was told that the train would stop in Green River, Wyoming, for about an hour while the train crew was being changed. I quickly called my Aunt Mildred and Uncle Karl Moedl, who had a drug store in Green River, to tell them I was going to be there. When we arrived, they met the train along with their two children, Martha Ann and Bob, and my grandmother Anderson. It was the first time I had seen them in six or seven years.

We had a short but nice visit before we had to leave. At the time I did not realize that nearly half of the troops on the train would either be casualties or not return at all from the Pacific. I was told that my grandmother cried all day when she found out that I had left California for the Pacific. I had lived with that dear, sweet soul for the first years of my life. Ours was a very close-knit family. She had seen her son go off to World War I and now her grandson was going off to fight in World War II.

chapter 4

Combat

THE TROOP TRAIN'S DESTINATION was San Francisco, where we boarded buses for Hamilton Army Air Field. Hamilton a was beautiful permanent base about twenty-five miles north of the Golden Gate Bridge, but sadly, it has been closed. When we got to Hamilton, we found many crews that had been waiting for two or three weeks for the Ford plant in San Diego to build B-24s to go to the Pacific Theater. Our B-24 was waiting for us, however, because it had been especially made with the new LAB bombing system. When we inspected the plane for the first time, it was a sobering experience. For the first time, we began to realize that this was the plane in which we were going to fight a war. What was going to happen to us in this plane? Was this where we were going to die?

We flew a couple of shakedown flights landing at Mather Army Air Field at Sacramento, California, which was the aerial port of embarkation for the Pacific. We were issued personal combat equipment that consisted of a .45-caliber pistol with a shoulder holster and ammunition, a steel helmet, and a blanket. We also received a small bag from the Red Cross that had a bar of soap, toothbrush and toothpaste, a razor and blades (which none of us needed), and a paperback book.

The day finally arrived when we were to take off for the south Pacific. We drew all our personal equipment and made ready. It just so happened that we had to abort because of bad weather. After four attempts we finally took off. By this time we each had four Red Cross packets. Fortunately the paperbacks were not all the same.

On February 14, 1945, at 3:00 A.M., we left Mather for John Rodgers Field, Honolulu, now Honolulu International Airport. It was a night flight so the navigator could use celestial navigation. As we left the mainland, looking ahead over the Pacific Ocean, it was completely black with not a light in sight. I turned around and looked back at the lights of San Francisco and wondered if I would ever see them again. The flight to Honolulu was uneventful and took fourteen hours and fifteen minutes. We took the remainder of the day for crew rest. Today's jets make the trip in about four hours.

The next morning we were scheduled for an early takeoff for Canton Island. We were number two for takeoff behind one of the crews with whom we had gone completely through training. They lost an engine on takeoff and cart-wheeled. All of the crew got out of the plane except the navigator. The top turret fell on top of him, pinning him into the aircraft and he was burned to death. The copilot, Lt. Donald Zech, and I had gone through pilot training and graduated together. Our flight was canceled for the day while they cleared the runway. The incident did not do a lot to raise our morale.

We took off on the morning of the seventeenth for Canton Island. It was a day flight and there were several islands in route where we could get radar and radio fixes. Canton was a pre-war refueling stop for commercial airlines' flights to Australia. It was nothing more than a sandy atoll. The highest point on the island was only about ten feet above the water and there was only one tree on the whole island. Canton was about 1,700 miles southwest of Honolulu. It took eleven hours and five minutes flying time en route.

We spent the night there and the morning of the eighteenth, we took off for Tarawa, which was almost due west of Canton. The flight only took six hours. At Tarawa we took a much needed two-day crew rest. The marine invasion had been over for several months, but the effects of the battle were still visible.

We went through some of the Japanese defensive positions. The Japanese machine-gun positions, facing the area where the marines were coming ashore, were very well constructed. They were built of coconut logs buried vertically in the sand with only a small opening for entry and another to fire through. There were two layers of coconut logs on top with sand bags and sand on top of them. In the center of the floor there was a deep round hole. The rest of the floor slanted into the hole so that any grenades that were thrown into the revetment would roll down into the hole. There was an opening toward the beach through which they fired machine guns. It was easy to understand why the marine casualties were so high and hard to understand how any of them made it to shore. The Japanese killed inside the revetments were never buried. The revetments were later covered over with sand by bull dozers. Rain had washed away some of the sand and there was a slight odor in the area.

One of the things that impressed me was a concrete blockhouse. The walls appeared to be two to three feet thick and able to withstand naval bombardment. On one of the walls there was a hole on the outside that appeared to be five to six feet in diameter. On the inside of the hole, it appeared to be only five inches across. It was apparent that during the invasion, one of the shells had struck the blockhouse, but did not penetrate the thick walls. Some of the Japanese got on top of the blockhouse. The only access to the roof was an outside staircase. The Japanese machine-gun fire was devastating. It was obvious that a number of marines died while trying to use the staircase to get to the top.

After inspecting the Japanese defenses we went for a swim. The water was crystal clear. As we walked along the beach, I stepped into the chest cavity of a dead Japanese.

After our crew rest we took off for Henderson Field on Guadalcanal on February 21. The flight took six hours and thirty minutes. I had read about the battle there and it was interesting to look down on Florida and Tologi Islands. When we landed, we found that there was still some Japanese activity on the island, so it was necessary to have the gunners guard our plane. After spending the night on Guadalcanal, we took off for Biak Island, which was off the west coast of New Guinea in the Netherland East Indies. En route we started having engine trouble so we diverted into Hollandia, which was on the northern coast of New Guinea. After engine repairs were made, we proceeded on to Biak on February 22.

General MacArthur's headquarters was in Hollandia at that time. An infantry colonel asked us for a ride to Biak where his unit was clearing the island of Japanese. He had been at a staff meeting at General MacArthur's headquarters. On the flight to Biak, he came up to the flight deck and told us that when one of his units came upon a Japanese bivouac area, they found the body of an American pilot who had been shot down. The Japanese had hung his body by the feet to a tree. They had butchered his body like a side of beef and were cutting off body parts to cook and eat, because they were starving.

When we arrived at Biak, we had to unload all our equipment. The plane was to be painted black with dark red numerals making them harder to see, as most of our missions were to be at night. The officers of the crew took all of our equipment to a tent in a replacement depot. The enlisted men went to a separate tent. They were large squad tents that could accommodate twelve to fifteen cots. The sides and flaps of the tent were all open because of the heat. Some of the people who had been there for a while told us how the Japanese threw grenades into the tents at night and bayoneted people in bed. This was true! A Japanese was killed in the area that very night. So they were not just trying to scare a bunch of green kids fresh from the States. That night, hearing jungle noises for the first time and the periodic machine-gun fire and screams, along with the stories I had heard, scared this twenty-year-old kid bad. I was determined they were not going to get me, so I put my .45 pistol right by my head and stayed awake all night, but just as the sky was beginning to get pink, I dropped off to sleep. I could not have been asleep more than what seemed like a few minutes when I woke up and discovered my pistol was gone! I never did find out what happened to it. I suspected it was an American who stole it. There was no problem replacing it. I got a new one from supply with no questions asked. When I wrote home about the incident, my Dad kidded me about going to war to protect him and having my gun stolen. He said he did not feel too safe with me guarding him.

While we were waiting to be assigned to a combat unit, one of the bombardiers from another crew and some of his gunners searched a cave that had been used by the Japanese. They found a mortar shell and brought it back to our tent. He decided he would try to defuse the shell to make a lamp out of it. He was beating on it. When I saw this, I rolled off my cot onto the ground and started yelling at him to get that thing out of there. He took the shell out of the tent area and continued trying to defuse it. Sadly it went off and he lost one hand plus several fingers on the other hand. Stupid? Yes.

While we were at Biak, we were sent to a replacement depot at Nadzab on the northeast end of New Guinea near the town of Lea. We got there late in the evening of the twenty-sixth. I was exhausted and did not take time to hang my mosquito bar; I just dropped on a cot and pulled a blanket over my head. It did not take long before I was covered with sweat. I tried to hang my mosquito netting but it was too late. Every mosquito within a mile radius came looking for me. I finally got the net hung, but the mosquitoes were inside the net and I did not have any bug spray. What a miserable night. The next night I tried to write a letter home, but under the light, I had a collection of every type of bug known to man and some that were not. I wondered why we fought so hard for New Guinea.

We never knew why we were sent to Nadzab. We were there about a week and had nothing to do except wait around the replacement depot for further orders. We did do a little sight-seeing. We walked to the town of Lea but there was next to nothing there. I was accused of having been there before because the natives had red hair. They were also red around the mouth caused by chewing a narcotic called betel nut.

One day a fighter pilot who had been shot down a couple of weeks before and was considered dead came into the area leading some wild, fierce-looking men. They had found the pilot some distance from Nadzab and brought him in. The pilot came through the area asking for coins or empty cans, anything, to give to the natives. He did not want full cans because the natives did not eat our kind of food, but made good use of the empty cans. Everyone gave every thing they had. It was good insurance if we were ever shot down and needed their help. The natives left with so much of their treasure, they could hardly carry it.

After about a week we were flown back to Biak. When we arrived back at the Biak replacement center, we went to the orderly room and were told they thought we were gone. I think it was another army screw up and we were sent to the wrong place.

The Philippines

In the early part of March, 1945, after another week in the Biak replacement depot, a crew flew in to pick us up to take us to Tacloben, Leyte. I never knew what happened to the B-24 we brought from the States. It must have been assigned to our counterpart, the 868th Bomb Squadron in the 13th Air Force, where half of the crews we trained with were assigned. Our crew was assigned to the 63rd Bomb Squadron, 43rd Bomb Group, 5th Air Force.

After we arrived on Leyte, the officers were assigned to a bamboo hut with a tent roof. The floor was about two feet off the ground and was covered with plywood. The porch had a railing about two feet high all around it. We slept on the porch because it was cooler but we still had to use mosquito nets. I never knew what happened to the crew that spent all of their time and effort building that hut, but I believe they were lost. Not too many crews completed their combat tour and returned to the States together.

Armed reconnaissance was the primary mission of the 63rd Bomb Squadron to isolate the battle fields and keep the Japanese from re-supplying their troops in the Philippines, especially those on Leyte. It was a 63rd Bomb Squadron crew that discovered the Japanese fleet approaching Leyte from the west, south of Leyte Island. They sank a Japanese destroyer and were able to pass the information to alert the navy as to the location of the Japanese fleet. This proved disastrous to the Japanese during the battle of Leyte Gulf.

By early 1945, there was very little left of the Japanese navy. The Allied forces had recaptured most of the islands the Japanese had taken in the early days of the war. I only saw one or two Japanese warships in all the time I spent searching the area between the Chinese mainland and the Philippines and Japan. The Japanese were trying desperately to survive. Their people were starving. The ships we were after were carrying supplies to the Japanese main islands. Supplies were being taken down the Yangtze River to Shanghai and from there (by staying close to the shore to avoid attack by bombers and submarines), they would make their way up to the Tsushima Straights between Korea and Japan, where they would make a dash across the Straights to Japan. We searched along the Yangtze and the area between mainland China and Japan for cargo ships that were taking mostly food and oil to Japan. The squadron also searched for Japanese shipping along the China coast from Borneo to the Formosa Straits.

We were only on Leyte a couple of weeks. The battle of Leyte Gulf was over, but the island was not secured and there was still Japanese ground and air activity. About a week before we arrived on Leyte, a Japanese transport plane entered the normal landing traffic pattern just at dusk. After it came to a stop, Japanese infantrymen jumped out shooting. Fortunately American infantrymen on airbase security killed all of them before they could do too much damage.

The bomb shelters in the area were pretty well constructed. They had a couple of layers of coconut logs with sandbags and dirt on top. During an air raid a bomb went off near the entrance of one of the shelters covering the entrance with dirt. Some time later it was discovered that one person was missing. After digging into his shelter, they found him, but the bomb blast concussion and being buried alive completely destroyed him mentally. He was never quite the same. A few days later the Japanese hit again. This time he was sitting in the eight-holer outhouse. He completely panicked and raised the cover and seat on one of the holes and jumped in. This time when they found him, he was about dead. You can imagine what he looked and smelled like after they fished him out. They took him to the nearby Leyte Gulf and made him get in the water. Every time he tried to get out, they threw rocks at him. After he was clean enough to get out, he was declared unfit and was sent home. We soon began to wonder which of us was crazy. He went home and we had to stay.

After we moved up to Ie Shima, one of the bombardiers rolled up in a blanket on his cot and covered his head. Even in that heat, he would not come out or talk to anyone or eat. After a couple of days he came out at night and tried to find something to eat. Combat rations were left where he could find them. The flight surgeon finally declared him insane and sent him home in restraint. These incidents may sound funny, but the human mind and body can only take so much. The *Admiral Mayo*, the troop ship I came home on, had a number of padded rooms for people who had lost their minds in combat.

We did some ferry work between Tachloben and Clark Field on Luzon, but did no combat flying while we were at Leyte. The squadron was preparing to move to Clark Air Base, but had to wait until the base and surrounding area was secured from the Japanese.

We finally received orders to fly a B-24 to Clark Air Base on Luzon Island in the Philippines, formerly old Fort Stotsenburg, at the end of March, 1945. Before we left Leyte, a Filipino guerilla asked if he could go to Clark with us because his home before the war was in Manila. He asked us to fly over Manila so he could see the war damage. As we flew over we could see parts of the city still burning. When we landed at Clark, we could only taxi in areas that had been cleared of land mines. The base was covered with Japanese aircraft that had been destroyed by air strikes.

In early April, we flew practice missions dropping 250- and 500-pound general purpose bombs on old Fort Drumm in Manila Bay. I studied about Fort Drumm at Texas A&M. The old fort was constructed after the Americans defeated the Spanish in 1898. It was a coast artillery fort made of reinforced concrete and was shaped like a battleship. It had naval gun turrets with large caliber guns to protect Manila Bay.

The Japanese had taken the fort after the fall of Bataan; however, it had been abandoned before that time and the guns were no longer serviceable. When the Americans retook Luzon, some Japanese took refuge in the old fort. They were little more than a nuisance. Periodically they would come out of the fort and fire machine guns at passing ships. I am sure we did little or no damage, and at best, we may have given the Japanese inside a few headaches. The old fort was finally taken by assault. Gasoline was poured down the air vents and ignited. I do not believe anyone went inside the fort to confirm that all the Japanese were dead.

When we settled in at Clark Air Base, the enlisted men's tent area was on an old Japanese runway, and the officer's area was on the side of the runway, which were both good for drainage. We found some old bomb and ammunition crates that we used to make a floor, a table, four chairs, and something to keep our clothes in. We were high and dry even in the hardest rains.

One night I woke up and saw a man standing in our tent. I eased my hand under a jacket I used for a pillow and pulled out my .45 pistol and was about to fire when the wind blew. The navigator, Bill Clark, had hung a shirt on a hanger. As close as we were to the Japanese, we agreed there would be no more shirts on hangers. Not only did it scare the hell out of me, it almost cost Bill his shirt. I can imagine the panic that would have been caused if everyone in the squadron were awakened by a gunshot in the middle of the night. The safest place to be would have been at least a mile away.

There was an artillery battery near us that was shooting at the Japanese in the areas of the Bambam River, just west of our squadron area. We had guard revetments around the perimeter that were manned after dark. Unfortunately the latrine was outside of the perimeter. It was funny to watch people going to the latrine with a flashlight in one hand and a .45 pistol in the other. They did not stay long.

One day we were watching artillery firing at the Japanese just west of our area, while two B-25s were strafing and bombing them. One of the B-25s crashed. The medics took an ambulance and rushed to the crash site to pick up the crew. When they returned, there were a couple of dozen Japanese walking in front of the ambulance. They had surrendered to the unarmed medics.

The medics did not know what to do with them and were trying to turn them over to anybody who would take them. They tried to turn them over to us because we were the nearest tent. We told them we would try to find someone to take them. We contacted an American infantry unit and were told to shoot them. That did not seem like a solution to us. There was no way we could shoot them. They were unarmed and looked like they were just happy to get out of the war. They certainly did not follow the Bushido medieval warrior code followed by all of the Japanese military. We finally turned them over to a Filipino military police unit. They picked them up in a GI truck. We never found out what happened to them. I hope they did not shoot them.

A few weeks later the artillery battery next to our squadron area moved and left an ammunition dump there. I never went near it and had no idea what had been left behind, until one day when I was out in front of our tent, the ammunition dump blew up. It knocked me to the ground and when I got up, there was a ringing in my ears I have never completely gotten over. I can still hear the roaring to this day. For the rest of my air force career, I had to have a hearing waiver to stay on flying status. It did not affect my flying that much because I just turned the volume on the radio up to drown out the roaring.

We got tired of the mess hall canned food, so when someone came along selling chickens, each of the officers bought one. They looked like they were nice and plump, but when you picked one up, you found out they were mostly feathers and darn little chicken. So we decided to let them grow for a while. We tied a piece of string to one of their legs and the other end to a tent stake. We left enough string so they could roost on the tent at night. We fed them cereal out of combat rations. We were gone most nights and did not realize they were beginning to crow and had become a nuisance until we began getting threats from our neighbors that if we did not do something about the chickens, they would. So we decided to kill and roast them, but we had become attached to them by that time and could not kill them. We were great warriors. We could bomb and kill Japanese but could not kill a chicken. One of our neighbors had been a farmer and he gladly volunteered to kill them to shut them up. We cleaned and dressed the chickens, tossing the entrails, heads, feet, and feathers in the dirt off to one side to be buried later. While we were roasting the chickens, some of the wildest looking people I have ever seen came up to the fire and joined us. They were about four and a half feet tall and wore practically nothing. They were decorated with paint and feathers and carried bows and arrows. The arrows had long jagged steel points, the kind you surely would not want to get shot with. They were Negritos, who spoke no English, and we spoke no Negrito, so we sat and grinned at each other. With sign language they let us know they wanted the chicken leftovers. We were glad to keep them happy, but were shocked to see them eat the intestines raw, as one might suck up spaghetti, dirt and all. After the "feast" they said something to us, grinned and disappeared into the night the way they came. They took the feathers, heads, and feet with them. I guess they were for the wives and kids. We were told later that they like Americans because we gave them things; they were not too happy with the Filipinos because they tried to tame them. They hated the Japanese because they killed them. We were told that the Japanese paid dearly for their mistreatment of the Negritos. Their forefathers were headhunters and they practiced their old ways on the Japanese.

There were lighter times during the war. Laughter was important after some of the things we saw. When the squadron was on Leyte, some-one caught a young monkey. They tied a string around the monkey's waist and the other end to a tent post. He was given freedom to run around the tent area and became quite tame. When we moved to Clark Air Base on Luzon, the monkey was moved, too; however, it was allowed to run free and became a real nuisance. I saw one of the men chasing it with a broom and threatening to kill it. Fortunately the monkey was faster and more agile than the chaser and managed to escape his fury. It seems the mon-key had gotten into the fellow's tent and demolished it. The monkey was getting completely out of hand, especially when crews came back from a mission and found that the monkey had taken liberties with their tents. Something had to be done about that *#%& monkey.

After we were at Clark Field for a few weeks, we scrounged some ma-terial and built an Officers' Club. It was nothing fancy, but there was no problem getting beer or Filipino whiskey. Only the brave or the desper-ate drank the whiskey. The monkey's owner was getting all kinds of threats against him and his monkey. There was a tree in front of the club, so while the club was being built, the monkey's owner built a little house for the monkey to live in. A collar was fastened around the monkey's waist and a string attached to his waist and to the house. Everything worked out fine until someone felt sorry for the monkey and took him some beer. The monkey thought it was great and gulped the beer down. The donor, be-ing a very generous person, and a little high himself, gave the monkey more beer. The first thing we knew, we had a well-oiled monkey on our hands. He would balance on his stomach on a limb. As if in slow motion, he would start to fall off going down head first but at the last second, he would reach up and catch the limb with his tail. If he fell backwards, he would catch the limb at the last second with his hand. He was a great source of amusement. He had redeemed himself and was everyone's friend, es-pecially if he had beer or whiskey. The next morning, however, he had a hangover and woe be unto the first person who went near that monkey until he had some of the "hair of the dog." Then he was everybody's buddy. Before long he had become a full-blown alcoholic. When we moved to Ie Shima the monkey went, too, and again, he had the freedom of the squad-ron area. In anticipation of the Japanese using poison gas in retaliation of the atom bomb attack, gas masks were issued. The monkey came into our tent one day, and I put on my gas mask and ran at the monkey, yelling. I did not know a monkey could move that fast. He took off and I do not think he was ever seen again, at least not around our tent.

In the Philippines the rats grow to the size of small dogs and can be quite destructive. One day one got loose in the squadron area. There was a lot of commotion with people chasing the rat. The rat ran into one of the tents and up the center pole. All of the brave warriors who were chasing the rat decided they were going to shoot it. So they loaded their .45 pistols with bird shot, which we had on hand for jungle survival. At the count of three, at least six fired. They all missed the rat, of course, and blew big holes in the top of the tent. In the confusion, the rat disappeared. It did not make much difference, until it rained.

While we were working to become "combat ready," one of the pilots who had finished his tour and was going back to the States told me in confidence how to survive the war. He said, "After takeoff, fly in the direction of your target area. When you are out of radar range, fly the approximate time the mission would take, then salvo your bombs in the ocean and return to Clark Air Base with a good fabricated story." He also said if we did not do it, we probably would not survive the war.

This man was a graduate of West Point whose father was an army general. Most of the men finished their tours as first lieutenants, but he had been promoted to captain and had received many decorations for valor in combat. By his own admission, he had never seen a shot fired in anger. At the time I could not believe what he was saying and thought if everyone was like that, we would never win the war. I also wondered how he could explain the truth to the families of those who did not come home. There is an old military saying: "Many brilliant military careers have been ruined by war." I was disgusted then and am disgusted now when I think about that coward. I do not know what ever happened to him. I cannot help but wonder what kind of commander he would make.

On April 15, we were pronounced "combat ready" and would join a bomber stream on an attack on Taihoku, Formosa (now Taipai, Taiwan). There were five other B-24s in the attack. The bomber stream took off at fifteen-minute intervals; we were the last aircraft in the stream. We carried homemade fire bombs, which were 55-gallon drums with tail fins attached, and filled with jellied gasoline using phosphorous grenades for fuses. The basic mission was to set the town on fire so that other B-24s flying at high altitude and carrying high explosives could drop from the light of our fires.

I had no idea what to expect. When we turned over the "initial point" (IP) to start the bomb run, the Japanese were ready for us. We were picked up by radar-controlled search lights. When we were in their beam, at least another dozen handheld search lights picked us up. It was like running down Main Street at high noon buck naked. During a bomb run the navigator stood next to the bomb bay door holding the bomb bay door switch in the open position. When the lights hit us, it startled him and he almost fell out of the plane.

All of a sudden the search lights went off for a short time. I found out after the mission that the gunners had thrown out a bunch of empty beer bottles. They made such a racket going down, I guess the Japanese took cover. The lights were not out for long though.

Then the heavy antiaircraft fire began. At night the bursts of antiaircraft fire are cherry red flashes. They were bursting all around us. The Japanese must have been firing every gun they had. When we were picked up by the radar search lights, I called the waist gunners and told them to throw out the rope (chaff or metal strips used to jam radar).

Sergeant Sedlow, one of the gunners, said, "I can't, Pat is kneeling over the camera hatch and has a canvas engine cover pulled over him."

I yelled, "Pat, get off the camera hatch."

He answered, "I'm talking to the Old Man, that will do more good than all the damn rope."

How we made it through all that fire and dropped our bombs without getting hit only God knows. Maybe Pat's talk with the "Old Man" did some good or maybe it was my rabbit's foot. I began to accept the thought that if all our missions were like that, there was no way we could survive the war and get home. The raids on Taihoku were scheduled to last three days to completely destroy the town. The follow-on B-24s dropping high explosives were canceled. While the air defense at the local airport was Japanese, the town was mostly Chinese. Someone in authority must have realized we were bombing our allies, not the enemy. The balance of the raids were canceled. I cannot say I was sorry.

The casualty rate was quite high. Occasionally planes would return to base with dead and wounded on board, but most of the casualties resulted from the plane failing to return at all. Since we were flying alone, no one would ever know what happened if a plane failed to return. We were told that three of the crews we trained with were killed on a disastrous daylight raid on Hong Kong. They were in formation when Japanese Zero's rammed them head on. At the last minute one of the Zeros pulled up, missing the plane he was to ram. That is the only crew that made it back to tell what happened.

Our planes were painted black with red numerals to make them

Out of the Night II, an all-black B-24M from the 63rd Bomb Squadron, the Seahawks, at Clark Field in May, 1945.

almost invisible to the enemy at night. We approached the targets at 1,500 feet to avoid enemy radar. We were there and gone before they had time to man their guns. Because we were so hard to see at night, we were seldom attacked by fighters. We were given a bomb load, takeoff time, and an area to search. From then on, we were on our own.

Nearly all of our missions from Clark were flown at a maximum altitude of 1,500 feet, which put us within range of small arms fire. Occasionally we would climb to 4,000 or 5,000 feet for secondary targets, but due to the extreme range of the missions, we could not use our fuel to climb to higher altitude unless we had favorable winds on our return from the target. To confuse them, we took the propellers out of synchronization on the bomb run so they could not rely on the sound of our engines to locate us.

In one way flying at low altitude worked to our advantage, in that we struck fast and disappeared into the night before they could man their guns. There was one big disadvantage, however. If we were hit by gunfire, there was little or no reaction time to cope with emergencies. We were too low to bail out and the B-24 was not built to withstand ditching. Had we tried to ditch into the ocean, we would have sunk almost immediately. One has to think that most of the crews who did not make it back ended up that way.

The LAB sight did not work too well in actual combat. We used it to search for targets and to line up on the target for the bomb run. The bombardier, Lt. Bob Burns, put masking tape vertically down the sighting glass and horizontally about the center of the glass to form a cross hair. He put his chin in the eyepiece of the Norden Bomb Sight. When the target went under the cross hair, he released the bomb. This system was called "fixed angle bombing" and was used as far back as World War I. The Norden Bomb Sight was designed for high-altitude bombing. We never used it on any of our missions.

Even on dark nights we could normally see the target from about a mile away. On a bright moonlit night we could locate ships by following the wake reflected on the water, which would trail for several miles behind the ships. After the target was located, we would maneuver to get the target into the moon's reflection on the water and make our bomb run, so we remained in the dark and they could not see us coming.

On all of our long-range missions we carried two gasoline tanks in the aft bomb bay. This left only the front to carry the bomb load. The bomb load varied with the target and the length of the mission; however, our normal bomb load for search missions was four to six 500-pound bombs or four 500-pound and two 250-pound bombs.

We had a critical moment on one mission. The bombs failed to drop when they were released by the bombardier. Our flight engineer, TSgt. Paul Stanfield, diagnosed the problem to be a bad electrical relay in the bomb bay. He decided to wire around the relay. The bomb bay doors were open and could not be closed. Because of the bombs, there was not enough room for him to wear a parachute and get to the relay. Hanging over the open bomb bay, he worked around the relay and we were able to continue our mission. Sergeant Stanfield was a dedicated and outstanding person.

We flew two missions to Canton, China; both were primary targets. We attacked University Air Drome and Tein Ho (White Cloud Air Drome), using 250-pound fragmentation bombs. The fuses protruded six to eight inches in front of the bomb to ensure a burst at ground level. This would allow bomb fragments to skip along the ground. The bombs were grooved similar to a hand grenade and to ensure better fragmentation, sometimes the bombs would be wrapped with barbed wire.

Hong Kong and Canton were easy targets to locate at night because Macau, across the bay, was Portuguese and did not black out. There were

Japanese fighters in the area, but they either did not see us or had no desire to attack. At White Cloud we strung our bombs across the runway just as a Japanese Zero was taking off to intercept us. Luckily one of the bombs hit him.

We flew a mission to bomb barracks in a Japanese military installation on Hainan Island. We dropped six 500-pound bombs. The tail gunner reported direct hits on every other barracks, which I considered pure luck. With more luck, I hoped the barracks we hit were full of Japanese soldiers.

At that time most of our missions were looking for Japanese shipping along the China coast and in the Yangtze River. We were authorized to attack any target without identification within twenty-five miles of mainland China and between Formosa and the mainland. It was called a blind bombing zone. One night this policy almost turned into disaster.

We picked up a target in the Formosa Straits and started our bomb run. At three miles out, the bombardier opened the bomb bay doors. I asked him if he had put the fuses in the bombs. He said, "No, turn off!" Just as we flew over the target, its identification code came on. It was an American submarine on the surface where it should not have been. Why did the bombardier fail to fuse the bombs? He normally did as soon as we leveled off after takeoff. This time for some reason, he failed to do so. Had he fused the bombs as usual, undoubtedly we would have killed a number of our own countrymen. Maybe someone was watching over the submarine crewmen. It is something to think about. One often wonders about such things in combat situations.

We had many missions in the Yangtze River from the Shanghai area to 250 miles upstream. We were looking for Japanese ships. There were no large war ships in the area. Occasionally we would find a fair-sized freighter, but most of the ships we found were 2,500- to 3,500-ton luggers the Japanese were using to haul supplies to Japan. Some carried antiaircraft weapons and could put up a fight, but at this point in the war, they did not have many warships left that were not guarding the homeland against invasion. Our B-29s were giving Japan a pretty good going over by then.

Early in the war an Italian luxury liner had been sunk in the Singapore area. After four years the Japanese raised the ship and were attempting to take it to Japan where it could be converted into an aircraft carrier. A great deal of effort was spent trying to find it as it was being moved up the China coast. On June 29, we were told to report to 5th Bomber Command for a briefing. A navy pilot was there who claimed he had found the liner in a river near Haiphong, French Indochina (now Vietnam). We were told to try to find and destroy it. He told us how to attack the liner down the river and was adamant that we should break right because all of the antiaircraft guns were on the left side of the river. We made our bomb run down the river as briefed. It was at night and we never saw the liner, so we made our bomb run down the river dropping our bombs on four small freighters docked along the river. The tail gunner reported good hits on all four. When we finished the run, we broke right. I do not think that sailor knew port from starboard because we broke into the Japanese antiaircraft fire. They put up a tremendous amount of fire power, but did not appear to come close. I had to laugh because we were so low we could see the Japanese gunners in their revetments. They had the lights on in the revetment so they could not possibly see us. However, when we returned to Clark, we found the Japanese did get a few lucky hits. They must have been firing to keep their commander happy. We had two bombs left after we broke away from the target area and were short of fuel. The radar operator reported a large target just off shore so we decided to attack it. It was a very dark night so we could not identify it visually because of the distance. Just after bombs-away, we could see that it was a blacked-out lighthouse. I doubt if it ever worked again because we had a perfect hit. During the Vietnam War, two friends who were pilots in the South Vietnamese Air Force, and who were just kids during World War II, remembered when the lighthouse off Haiphong was destroyed. They were both from North Vietnam, but had defected to the South.

I wonder how many B-24s Tokyo Rose reported shot down that night. Tokyo Rose was an American working for the Japanese. She was a disc-jockey who broadcast propaganda to the Americans to discourage and depress the troops by reporting exaggerated losses. We listened to her because she played good American music, but her commentaries gave us a laugh. After the war she was sent to prison.

Later in the war, when Shanghai was a shipping hub, the Japanese converted some old ships that were used for laying communications cables. They removed all of the superstructure and added three or four tiers. Each tier was covered with different caliber antiaircraft weapons. They made flak ships and decoys of them. Five of them were spread across the mouth of the Yangtze River. I believe they had a lot to do with our high casualty rate. No one made it home to tell about them.

One night we were working the Yangtze when I looked out the window and saw a Japanese Zero flying formation with us with all his lights on. We had been warned about this and told not to fire because they were willing to sacrifice one plane to shoot us down. The tail gunner could not see any Japanese planes above us. The Japanese was not suicidal because he moved away when we got near a cloud. If we had fired at him and not killed him with the first burst, he could have rammed us. Since his guns were facing forward, we felt he could not hurt us, but if he turned toward us, the gunners were cleared to fire. We picked up a ship in the mouth of the river and began our attack. When we opened our bomb bay doors, the Zero pealed off and left. We did not realize at the time that we were about to attack one of the flak ships. He must have been forwarding our altitude and heading to the ship. We were about to be ambushed.

When we flew over the ship, the Japanese were ready. I could not see out the windshield because there was such a wall of fire in front of us. At that time the number three engine quit, and I assumed it was from the gunfire. I thought, "This is it." I did not have time to immediately survey the damage or pray. After we came out the other side of the fire, the number three engine came back on. We never knew why. The tail gunner, SSgt. Johnny Mullauer, had a real ring-side seat and he said he felt the Japanese had something personally against him and were shooting directly at him. He did report that one of the bombs went off between ten and fifteen feet from the boat. A near miss such as this can put a great deal of water pressure against the ship's hull and can sometimes cause more damage than a direct hit. I think we sank the flak ship because two days later, it was gone. We did not stay around to see if it sank, so we could not claim a ship. We were just glad to get away. The tail gunner is convinced we had an extra crew member on board that night. Once again God stepped in and decided our fate. When we got back to the base and inspected the plane, there was only very minor battle damage. Eventually all of the flak ships disappeared.

We flew a total of ten missions searching for Japanese ships in the Yangtze River. If no ships were found, our secondary target was normally the docks and warehouses on the Whang Po River, which adjoined the Shanghai Turning Basin. Across the Whang Po from the docks was a Texaco tank farm that we also went after without much luck. I flew over the tank farm after the war was over. There were a lot of bomb craters, but only one tank had been destroyed. Occasionally there were two or

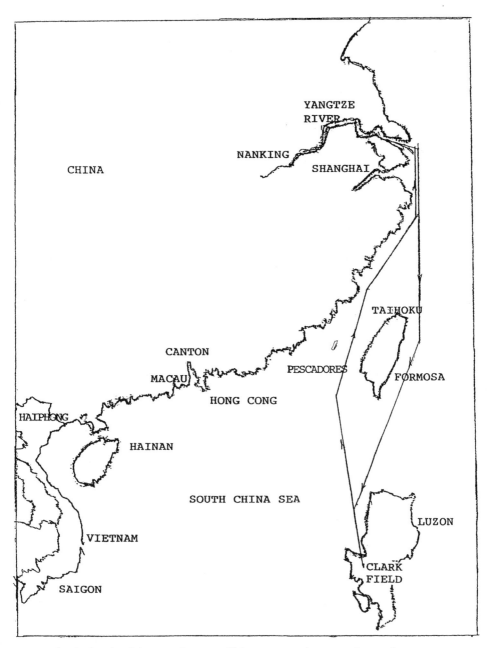

Author's sketch of the usual route of his Yangtze River search. He flew ten such missions. The average flight time was 18 hours, 15 minutes.

three B-24s from the 63rd Bomb Squadron working the Yangtze River at the same time; however, our takeoff times were staggered by an hour. If the plane ahead of us had not found a ship, we could see a great amount of gunfire over Shanghai. We knew they were going after the secondary targets. If we did not find a ship to attack, we counted the minutes until it was our turn to go into all that gunfire. One night we made a bomb run on a secondary target, the dock area. We were at about 1,500 feet when our bombs hit something that caused a secondary explosion. The plane rocked and bucked fiercely, but finally settled down with no damage. We never did know what we hit.

We had trouble getting the gunners in the rear of the plane to wear their emergency survival equipment in the target area. It was understandable that on such long flights, they would take it off while en route to the target and on the way home when we were out of danger. But one night in the Shanghai area there was a lot of gunfire, and in the confusion, one of us in the cockpit inadvertently hit the emergency alarm bell giving the signal for bail-out. I was calling, *"Don't bail out! Don't bail out!"* on the interphone, but it was too late. The gunners had taken off their headsets and were trying to find their Mae West life jackets and parachutes in the dark. We finally got someone still on the interphone to stop the fiasco. We never had any more trouble getting them to wear their emergency equipment in enemy territory.

The B-24 did not have a toilet on board. On our long missions, one was badly needed. One of the waist gunners had to go, so he used an empty ration box. After he finished he opened the bomb bay door and threw the box out. When the box hit the slip stream, it came right back into the plane and hit the thrower. What a mess!

On June 20, our secondary target was the marshalling yard at Nanking. We flew up the Yangtze River looking for ships but found none, so we dropped our bombs on our secondary target. There were some handheld search lights, but they passed over us and evidently did not see us. There was some minor antiaircraft fire, but it was not effective. We did not have enough fuel to go back down the river, so we flew a direct route back to Luzon. About a third of the way across China, it began to get daylight. I was enjoying the sights of rural China, seeing how the people lived in small communities, when a Japanese Zero fighter came into view below us. There was a thin overcast, so we climbed above it; he climbed above it. We descended; he descended. We did that several times but he made no attempt to attack. Finally he left, because of fuel, I suppose. The entire flight took twenty hours. It was questionable if we had enough fuel to get back to Clark, so we landed at an emergency strip at Laoag on north Luzon for fuel.

On one flight in the Yangtze, we found a good-sized freighter. On our first run the bombardier dropped a 500-pound bomb off the stern. It must have caused some damage because the freighter came to a stop. It must have had a charmed life because the bombardier made several more runs, but never did hit it. We were at low-level skip bombing and he bounced one bomb over the ship. I was flying, and after we ran out of bombs, I told the gunners we would make another pass at the ship and they were to strafe it. I was so intent on destroying the ship that I got "target fixation" and was diving directly at the ship. If the nose gunner had not yelled, I would have rammed it. I reacted just in time to pick up a wing as we flew over the mast. This can happen when you are so angry and intent on hitting the target, you will fly right into it.

One night one of the crews found the Italian luxury liner that we tried to find near Haiphong, French Indochina. The Japanese were trying to get it to Japan. They got it as far as Shanghai before it was discovered. The crew decided to skip bomb it. Just as the bombardier warned that they were too low, the plane hit the water, broke in half, and sank almost immediately. An inflated life raft came to the surface, the two waist gunners and the radar operator, who was a second lieutenant, also surfaced next to the life raft. They climbed in. The radar operator's face was very badly cut up. They found a first-aid kit in the raft and the gunners taped his face back together with bandaids as best they could. They paddled ashore and hid in a rice paddy until it was daylight. The gunners felt they had to get some help because the radar operator was in such bad shape. They left the radar operator in the rice paddy and went looking for help. A couple of hours later a group of Japanese soldiers came down a nearby road carrying the two gunners heads on poles. The radar operator stayed in the rice paddy until dark and then started walking west away from Shanghai. He eventually made it to Kungming, about 1,500 miles away, which was under Chinese and American control. After he got away from Shanghai, he got help from the Chinese. The Japanese mainly held the China coast and some of the larger cities inland. The trip took almost four months. By then the squadron had moved to Ie Shima and the war was over. He was airlifted back to the squadron. I knew him before he went down but his face was so badly scarred, I hardly recognized him. He told me his story.

Our shack on Ie Shima.

TSgt. Paul Stanfield,
flight engineer.

Lt. Don Zech, classmate in pilot training.

Left to right: SSgt. Bill Lee, nose gunner; TSgt. Red Melancon, radio operator; SSgt. Johnny Mullauer, tail gunner; and TSgt. Casey Sypnewski, radar operator.

通 告

誠摯的中國朋友們：

　　凡在左袖上帶有這些徽章的都是諸位的朋友。他們就是美國航空員，前來幫助你們把那可恨的日寇驅逐到中國國境以外。

　　諸位或者曾經看過這張紙上端的徽章。過去的五年之間在　蔣委員長指揮之下作戰的美國航空員，就是佩帶着這種徽章。

　　其他的美國航空隊員現在必來幫助　貴國抗戰。他們在左袖上所佩帶的，就是下面兩種徽章。對於佩帶這三種之中任何一種徽章的外國人，於有必要時，請求諸位儘量地加以援助。他們就是諸位的朋友。諸位因援助他們而用掉銀錢，不論多少美國政府必將全額償還。

　　　　　　　　　　　　　　　　　　美軍總司令佈

Blood chits that were carried while flying over China.

We all carried "blood chits" with Chinese and American flags displayed on them, and written in Chinese was a message that offered $10,000 in American money to whomever helped return the carrier of the chit back to Allied control. The Japanese found out about the offer and offered $15,000, if the carrier was turned over to the Japanese. We had been warned to stay away from anyone in the Shanghai area because we would be turned over to the Japanese. The Japanese paid off in Japanese-printed American invasion money, which they intended to use when they invaded the United States.

One day while I was sitting on my cot, someone came through the tent area announcing that President Roosevelt had died. Everyone seemed to be devastated by the news. All of the troops had great faith in our leaders, Winston Churchill and Franklin Roosevelt. The new president, Harry Truman, was an unknown factor at that time. We did not know what to expect, but as the war progressed, he, too, gained our confidence, especially after he ordered the atomic bomb dropped on Japan ending the war.

While we were at Clark Field in the Philippines, local women washed our clothes if we provided the soap. Strong GI soap was available, but after having been boiled in that soap a few times, the clothes began to look pretty tacky. We cut the sleeves and legs out of a couple of uniforms to wear around the squadron and keep a little cooler. No one cared how we looked. We were too far ahead in combat zones to be near any headquarters where someone would get excited if they saw the way we dressed. After we moved to Ie Shima, we had to wash our own clothes. We built a fire and filled an empty ammunition can with water and GI soap, and let them boil until we hoped they were clean. Then we rinsed and hung them on the side of the tent to dry.

In general the food in the squadron mess was pretty good considering it was all either canned or dried. It was not too well prepared and the daily menu was pretty much the same. We were at the mercy of the navy. They issued all the food since they brought it on ships under their control. All the fresh food came on refrigerated transports and they either kept it themselves or issued it to the top brass. I am one of the few people who came out of the Pacific Theater who likes Spam. We got a lot of it.

Our main problem was eating while we were on the long missions. Before the mission the gunners were issued a case of "ten-in-one" rations. They were designed for one meal for ten men. The case consisted of a large can of raw bacon. Of course we had no way to cook the bacon, so the gunners took it back to their tent after the mission. There were ten

Example of the 15,000 leaflets dropped on the mission to Nanking, June 20, 1945.

The crew on Ie Shima. Back row, left to right: Sgt. Bill Lee, Lt. Allan Stein, Lt. Bill Canevari, Lt. Bill Clark, Lt. Bob Burns, Sgt. Paul Stanfield. Front row, left to right: Sergeant Blacky, Sgt. Pat Dowling, Sgt. Ken Cyr, Sgt. Emery Melancon, Sgt. Johnny Mulhauer.

individual ration boxes that consisted of one small can of a prepared meal, a can of three hard crackers, a packet containing three cigarettes and a book of matches, a can opener, a packet of lemon powder to mix with water that tasted like battery acid, some toilet paper, and, for energy, a chocolate bar. Unfortunately, the chocolate bar was made of something that would not melt in the heat. It would not melt in your mouth either. The prepared food was made to be heated and, of course, we had no way to heat it during a mission. There is nothing like cold bacon and eggs. We usually ate on the way home from a mission. Going to the target, we were preparing ourselves for the mission and were too tense. In the target area we were too busy. By the time things settled down and we were on the road home, we were pretty hungry.

On the long trip back to Clark Air Base from Shanghai, we would go out to sea to get away from any fighters in the area. We did not go down the Formosa Straights because by then it was daylight and there was too good a chance of being jumped by fighters. So we went east of Formosa out of fighter range and then south back to the Philippines. There was an island in the Formosa Straights between Formosa and mainland China called Pescadores. Some of the crews heading back after a mission would strafe it. It had absolutely no tactical value. They did it just for sport. Finally the Japanese put some antiaircraft guns there and some of the planes would come back with battle damage. In one instance we came in and parked next to a plane that had been badly damaged after strafing Pescadores. The nose was covered with blood. There was a young airman fighting for his life in the nose with a young medic frantically trying to save his life. Beneath the plane was a doctor, a former pediatrician, chatting with people who had gathered to see what had happened. I will never forget the anger and disgust I felt at the sight. That young airman gave his life for nothing more than some irresponsible pilots enjoying a sport of shooting up that island. It served no purpose in winning the war.

Johnny Mullauer, the tail gunner, and Paul Stanfield, the flight engineer, liked to fly so they would sometimes take one of the pilot seats and fly us home. This would give either Bill Canevari or me a chance to take a break. I thought this was a good idea because if both of the pilots were incapacitated, they could get the airplane within bail-out distance of home.

Unlike combat crew training and the high-altitude missions in Europe, we did not receive a formal pre-takeoff and weather briefing before each mission. We flew regardless of bad weather conditions. We were given a search area, bomb load, takeoff time, and occasionally some special item or warning. It was all on a very informal basis.

After we landed from a mission, we dropped by the intelligence officer's tent where we critiqued the mission—though sometimes we met just under the wing of the airplane. We stopped by the medic's tent and were given a shot of whiskey to calm us down and help us sleep. After one very tough mission we did not settle for the usual one shot and took the whole bottle and slept well. The medics did not complain. I guess they thought we earned it.

There were American submarines stationed east of Formosa to rescue crews who had to ditch or bail out. This happened to one of the crews. They ditched near a submarine and were picked up, transferred to a Catalina flying boat, and were flown back to Clark. We were briefed on the general location of the submarines. We were also told to stay away from the center of the island of Formosa (Taiwan) because the natives were headhunters.

On July 16, we got a call from 5th Bomber Command that we were to put on our best uniforms because we were going to transport some VIPs to Okinawa. When we got to the flight line, the "VIPs" were two Chinese house boys with two large sacks of rice and a foot locker with some general's silverware and dishes. There was also a major in class "A" uniform who was wearing a val-pack, a .45-caliber pistol and an M-1 carbine. He was also carrying a bathroom sink! Probably the general's aide.

We landed at Yontan Field on Okinawa. There was heavy fighting there, but it was a little south of Yontan. We found that we were required to go to Ie Shima, an island off the west coast of Okinawa. A short runway had been built out of pierced steel planks (PSP) for fighters who were to protect ships supporting the invasion of Japan. When we taxied off the runway, mud was ankle-deep. We dropped the VIP and were fed by the Red Cross. We were told we were the first heavy bomber to land on Ie Shima since the invasion. Ernie Pyle, the famous war correspondent, had been killed near there a couple of weeks before. The infantry was still cleaning out Japanese snipers. We returned to Clark after our "important flight" to ferry the VIP.

Before we moved to Ie Shima, the military police started their move first. This made it necessary for the gunners to guard the planes. One night the gunners were being transported to the flight line on the back of a truck. A Japanese stepped out of the weeds into the headlights of the truck and the gunners started blazing away with their rifles. He took off running down the road still in the headlights of the truck. They finally killed him, but when they checked the body, there was not a bullet hole in him. They had run over him with the truck. It made you think of the Keystone Kops. We all thought he probably wanted to surrender but the gunners never gave him a chance. This little event made me think twice about the shooting ability of the gunners and I hoped they were better at shooting down fighters.

On July 23, the 63rd Bomb Squadron was ordered to move to Ie Shima. There was still fighting on Okinawa, while a landing strip was being prepared from which attacks could be launched against the Japanese homeland. All the squadron tents were struck and loaded on trucks along with all squadron equipment. No one in charge gave the troops much consideration because all of the packaged combat rations were on the trucks. They were driven by convoy over the mountains just north of Bataan to the ocean on the west coast of Luzon. From there they were to be loaded on navy landing ship tanks (LSTs) and taken to Ie Shima.

I was directed to lead the convoy. I had a Jeep and driver; there were ten trucks in the convoy. I assigned two enlisted men armed with automatic weapons to ride on each truck as there was still some sniping in the area. I carried my .45 pistol and a submachine gun. The convoy did not get started until late afternoon. Just at dusk we started up the zig-zag pass when our headlights flashed on a "caution sign" I shall never forget. On top of a post there was a Japanese head wearing a steel helmet; the flesh was falling from its cheeks and there were red reflectors in its eye-sockets. Below the head there were two crossed thigh bones with flesh dangling from them. If that will not put you on the alert, nothing will. After we got through the pass and to the ships, I left the trucks and enlisted men. I had to go back to Clark that night the same way we came. What a spooky ride that was.

Ie Shima

The next day we struck our tent, loaded everything we owned on one of the B-24s, and flew to Ie Shima, arriving in the early afternoon. The Corps of Engineers had constructed a new, long coral runway. After we landed, the squadron operations officer came by and told us to unload the plane and stand by. A couple of hours later a bomb service truck came by and started loading 500-pound bombs on the plane. The operations officer came by again, and told us to stand by. Then a fuel tank truck came by and started to refuel the plane. By then it was getting dark. We had not been told we were going out on a mission, but it did not take a genius to figure it out. The operations officer came back with a truck and told the enlisted men to put all our equipment on the truck and to stand by. He said a crew in the new squadron area would take care of our equipment. The officers were to go with him in his Jeep while the enlisted men were to remain with the plane. He took us to a tent in the new squadron area. Boxes were stacked up to form a flat surface on which to stretch out a map. The map was lighted by a kerosene lamp. The whole thing was like a scene right out of the movies. We were briefed on our target area and told to be prepared to take off as soon as possible. Our target was to search for Japanese shipping in the Inland Sea near the Japanese Kyushu Island. The fact that we were going to attack Japan itself added to the spooky briefing. We were told to expect much stronger opposition. There were large war ships protecting the Empire. We were given the operating radio frequencies for the Black Widow night fighters, who were to come to our rescue in the event we were attacked by Japanese interceptors. I commented that the crew had not eaten in two days and asked if there was any food available. I was told no, but by the time we got back, the messing facilities would be up and we would get a hot meal.

After takeoff it was only about a three-hour flight from Ie Shima to Japan. This was welcome after the long missions we had been flying to get to the targets from Clark. We entered the Sea of Japan through the Bungo Suida (Straits) between the Japanese islands of Kyushu and Shikoku. We could see a lot of Japanese air activity; however, they did not attack. Either they did not see us or they had other missions. Some of the Japanese fighters came quite close and we expected them to attack, so I tried to contact the Black Widows, but had no luck. We were on our own. We found several small targets, but were briefed to look for larger targets. We finally found a large target, but it was impossible to determine what it was from the radar return. We started our bomb run and as we approached the target, a tremendous amount of gunfire came up. Our target turned out to be one of the few remaining Japanese warships. I caught a quick glimpse of the ship's super structure as we passed over it. The bombardier released all six of our 500-pound bombs in one salvo. We never knew if we hit it or not. We were at about 1,500 feet. There was a lot of noise, but the tail gunner could not confirm a hit. Since we did not have any more bombs and were sure the Japanese were alerted to our presence, we withdrew the same way we entered the Inland Sea. We had no major battle damage, so we returned to Ie Shima.

When we returned, we found that everything we owned was dumped in a mud hole with a tent pulled over the top. We asked about the hot meal and were told there was none. The mess tent had not been erected as yet. If that major squadron commander worked for me in Vietnam and could not take better care of his troops than that, he would have been in serious trouble. I realize it was necessary to move the messing facilities, but he should have provided combat rations. We gave up on the squadron and started looking for something to eat. We stopped by a Corps of Engineers' mess hall and asked the black mess sergeant if he could help us. He said they were through serving. But when we told him we had just returned from a mission to Japan and had not eaten in three days, he said, "You boys come on in, I'll feed you." Thanks to him, we finally got our good hot meal.

There was still a lot of fighting going on in southern Okinawa but only mopping up in the north. Ie Shima was invaded by the 77th Infantry

Division on April 14, 1945. This was the same Division that the "Lost Battalion" was assigned to in World War I. By the time we arrived the island was secure with the exception of some minor sniping. All of the bodies of the Japanese killed in the battle had not been buried. We set up our tents and began to get things in order. Fox holes had been dug through the area and we were bombed almost every night. Most of the Japanese raids were against ships supporting the battle on Okinawa, but they still managed to give us some trouble from time to time. We seldom went to a fox hole when the alert was sounded because we thought they were just after the ships. I never knew I could move so fast as I did when a bomb hit nearby. We kept our steel helmets handy under our cots. After one raid we found the navigator, Bill Clark, sitting on his cot. He seemed dazed. When we questioned him, we found that when I pulled my helmet out from under the cot, I clipped him on the chin. Another time, while we were building a floor out of scrap wood, the bombardier forgot where he kept the nails until he jammed his helmet on his head.

We had the best tent or shack in the squadron. One of the squadron staff members asked if he could move in with us. He traded two cases of beer to the marines for enough material to build the frame for the tent with screen sides and a screen door. We used a tent for the roof. After we had completed our shack, the marines came back asking for one of the kegs of nails back, so he traded one of the kegs for a case of beer. What a trader. After the war he became a preacher in Henderson, Texas. When one of the lieutenants finished his combat tour, he gave me his air mattress and sheets made out of an old parachute. Compared to the rest of the people in the squadron, I lived like a king. However, I would pump it up at night when I went to bed, but by morning, the air had all leaked out. At least it kept me from sleeping late.

Another night there was an air raid alert. I did not pay much attention until the first bomb went off. It was close enough to get my attention. The next bomb was even closer. I was determined at that point that I would be in a fox hole before the next one hit. I dove head first into the nearest one. Some poor guy was laying on his back watching the antiaircraft fire. I hit him dead center in the stomach with my steel helmet. There was a gasp for air and a groan. By the time he came around, the air raid was over and I had left. A couple of years later I was in a base operations somewhere, filing a clearance, when a sergeant kept watching me. I was wearing my old jacket with the 63rd Bomb Squadron patch. He came over to me and said he recognized the patch, but could not remember me. We introduced ourselves and started talking about Ie Shima. He told me about the time during an air raid that someone hit him in the stomach with a steel helmet. I stuck out my hand and said, "Meet your attacker." We had a good laugh and parted. I never saw him again.

In late July the fighter group stationed on Ie Shima took off on an interdiction mission against a Japanese air field on Kyushu Island where most of the Japanese kamikazes were stationed. En route between Kyushu and Ie Shima, the American fighters met a large group of kamikazes headed for the ships supporting the Okinawa operation. The Japanese pilots had only a minimum amount of training. They were taught to take off, fly straight and level, and dive into American ships. They were no match for the Americans. All of the Japanese planes were shot down. When the fighters returned from the "turkey shoot," they flew individually down the runway at a very low altitude doing a victory roll for each Japanese they had shot down. Several did two or three rolls. They had saved many American lives that day.

The primary mission for the 63rd Bomb Squadron after our move to Ie Shima was to isolate the battle field on Okinawa and to blockade Japan by preventing shipping from China and Korea from reaching Japan. Our main areas for this purpose were the Tsushima Straits Eastern Channel between Tsushima Island and Kyushu and Honshu, as far north as the Sea of Japan and as far south and east as Kyushu Island and Shikoku Island to include the Inland Sea.

On July 27, we were assigned a search area in the Sea of Japan along the north coast of Honshu. We found only small targets that we attacked with unknown results. On July 31, we went back to the Inland Sea area again, but all we could find were small targets. Fortunately we never saw the ship on this mission so maybe we did some damage after all, but no proof we could claim.

On August 6, we flew a mission into the Tsushima Straits (Eastern Channel); we found nothing. By this time in the war, most of the Japanese shipping had been destroyed. On August 10, we were to search the same area but were told to remain clear of the west coast of Kyushu Island in the area of Nagasaki. No one knew why. When we got into the target area, we started searching along the coastline as the remaining Japanese ships tried to hug the coastline in an attempt to hide from us. As we approached Nagasaki, we ignored the warning and flew over the town at about 1,500 feet. We had no idea what had happened. I thought it had been a B-29 firebomb raid. The atom bomb was dropped about ten o'clock

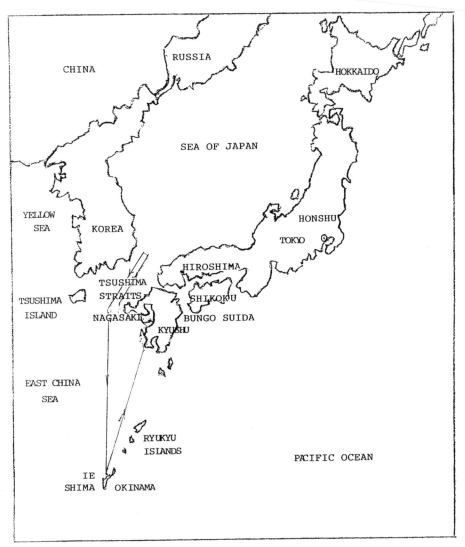

Author's sketch of his flight path over the Tsushima Straits. The average flight time was 11 hours, 10 minutes.

in the morning and we flew over Nagasaki between 8 P.M. and 9 P.M. There were a lot of fires and as we flew over, there was some turbulence from the fires. I do not remember how I heard about the atom bomb. The people in the States knew about it long before we did. We thought the B-29s might be back, so we left the area to continue our mission.

We found two targets close together. In the moonlight they looked like PT boats. We began the bomb run, releasing only one 500-pound bomb. The bomb came close enough that both boats stopped. We made three more runs releasing one bomb on each run. In the moonlight it appeared that both boats had severe damage and that one was sinking. They started flashing lights to shore and were answered from shore. We suspected they were asking for help. In a short time, we picked up a target coming from shore at high speed. We had two bombs left so we left the immediate area, but watched the boats on radar and in the moon's reflection on the water. We waited until all three boats were together and we made another bomb run. Just at bomb release, the third boat fired a rocket salvo at us. Rockets went all around us, but thank God none hit. We believed the third boat was taking off survivors and the first two boats were sunk. When we returned to Ie Shima, the ground crews were celebrating the end of the war. I remember saying, "It's too bad no one has told the Japanese about it." It was a false armistice.

Two days later we were searching the Tsushima Straits when at 9 P.M., our radio operator, TSgt. Emory Melancon, received a radio message telling us to "continue searching, an important message to follow." At 9:30 P.M. he received a message telling us to "salvo our bombs and return to base. THE WAR IS OVER."

chapter 5

World War II in Retrospect

NO ONE ON THE CREW SAID A WORD. There was no feeling of elation. There was no celebration or any comment by the crew about the war being over. We simply salvoed our bombs and returned to Ie Shima. Even after we landed, there was no celebration. We were just too exhausted. I think we were afraid to believe it in case there was some mistake and it was not true. We returned to our tents in the squadron area and went to bed. It took a few days for it to sink in that the war was really over and we would be returning home. I do not think I really realized it until I was actually on the way home.

When we were on our way over to the Pacific area, we looked upon it all as a great adventure until we actually got into combat. We had to try to adjust to the loss of comrades and the death and destruction and gunfire, but one never really adjusts to war. One only hopes he can struggle through it all somehow. We were so very young, but by the time it was all over, we felt very much older. Going from a combat environment to a peace time one is an emotional adjustment that does not just happen because one hears the words.

During our combat tour we were credited with sinking six Japanese ships, plus two probably sunk and three more damaged. We were in eight battles or campaigns: Leyte, Luzon, Borneo, China (Formosa), China (Mainland), Ryukyus (Okinawa and Ie Shima), Inland Sea (Japan), and the Air War over Japan. We flew 347 combat hours between April 15 and August 10, 1945. In May we flew nine missions that totaled 140 combat hours or almost sixteen hours per mission; nearly all were at night. Needless to say this was a heavy load to carry. Many times we landed after seventeen- or eighteen-hour missions, ate a meal, and went to bed. The next morning we began to get ready to go back out the next afternoon. On one occasion Bill Canevari went to sleep en route to the target and was so exhausted that I could not wake him up when we got into the target area and were getting ready to attack a Japanese freighter. It was not until we started strafing and the noise from the 50-caliber machine gun just above his head finally woke him up. The number of missions flown in May was due mainly to heavy casualties. The squadron got down to five B-24s and just a few crews. Normally a bomb squadron has seventeen aircraft and twenty-four crews. However in July, we began receiving aircraft and crews that were being diverted from Europe to build our squadron up to full strength.

Unfortunately, all of the crew did not get to come home. On July 27, 1945, SSgt. Raphael (Speedy) Sedlow, one of the waist gunners, volunteered to fly a mission with Lieutenant Kern's crew. At 1 *a.m.* Lieutenant Kerns sent a strike report that they had sunk a Japanese tanker and were continuing their search. They never came back. We never knew what happened, but suspected they were shot down.

Speedy was a quiet and well-mannered person, so much so, that I was afraid he would fold when the going got tough, but he never did. He was from Detroit. I had an opportunity to visit with his mother after the war. She lived all alone in a small three-room apartment over a store in a rather poor part of town. He was an only son. She had his picture on a table with his Purple Heart beside it. Like Speedy, she was soft spoken and polite. I wished her well and have thought of her often. Staff Sergeant Sedlow will be remembered, as his name is engraved on a column in the Punch Bowl National Cemetery in Honolulu, along with others killed in the Pacific whose bodies were never recovered.

Technical Sergeant Casimer L. (Casey) Sypniewski volunteered to fly with another seasoned crew as a spare radar operator. He had gone through training with the regular radar operator and they were personal friends. All of our flights were at night; however, this mission was flown during the day time. The target area was along the French Indochina coastline.

At about 10:30, they spotted an enemy convoy of four large merchant ships protected by three destroyers, two destroyer escorts, and one light cruiser. They made a low-level attack on the largest merchant ship at about 300 feet dropping three bombs. But the bombs were duds. Every gun in the convoy was shooting at them. As they pulled away, the tail gunner was wounded in the leg and the tail section of the plane was riddled with bullets. They turned around for a second attack, this time releasing their remaining five bombs. Two of the bombs were hits followed by a violent explosion. As the crew looked back, they saw the ship list sharply to port and it was belching black smoke. The Japanese guns destroyed all of the plane's trim tabs and partial elevator control.

There was a Japanese airfield nearby and as the plane pulled up after the second attack, two Japanese fighters attacked the plane head-on and killed the copilot. The regular radar operator went back to the tail to replace the wounded tail gunner. The fighters turned and attacked from the rear. Technical Sergeant Sypniewski said he was watching his friend when he was hit in the head and killed instantly. The waist gunners were also wounded on the second pass.

The Japanese fighters continued their attacks knocking out the bomber's number three engine and hit number one and two engines. They also destroyed the upper gun turret. One of the fighters was hit and was trailing smoke when last seen. The remaining fighters continued to attack until the B-24 escaped into cloud cover.

The hydraulic system was destroyed, the radio was shot out, and a fuel line was damaged and leaking fuel into the bomb bay; however, it was repaired. After six hours with only two engines operating, they made it back to Clark Air Base. The landing gear was cranked down manually, but on the landing the right gear collapsed causing the plane to turn violently to the right.

Technical Sergeant Sypniewski received severe back injuries on the landing and was taken to the hospital, which was located in some pre–World War II hangers at Clark. I visited him there to see if he needed anything and to check on his progress. He, too, was from Detroit and I saw him seven or eight years after the war and he could hardly walk because of his back.

While I was visiting him in the hospital at Clark, I noticed a little boy and little girl; they appeared to be about six or seven years old. Both were missing both hands just above the wrist. I asked the nurse if they had gotten a grenade. She said, "No, a Japanese officer offered them some candy and when they held out their hands for the candy, he cut them off with a samurai sword." It made me sick to see those children and to think of their future. Even after all these years, when I think of those children and how they had to go through life, it still haunts me.

During the Japanese occupation of the Philippines, the people were treated harshly by the Japanese soldiers. A large portion of the food crops were confiscated and shipped to Japan. This was especially hard on the children. After the American invasion they would gather in groups around the mess hall garbage cans with large cans with wire handles attached, awaiting bits of food to be thrown out by our men. More than once I have seen soldiers empty their mess kits with a complete meal into the children's buckets and walk away hungry. It was quite a contrast to the way the Japanese treated them.

The Atom Bomb

I have heard and read many times that the Americans should not have dropped the atomic bombs on Japan, that it was inhumane, and that the Japanese would have surrendered anyway because they were starving and beaten. All imports to Japan had been stopped by our air and sea blockade. Those with that philosophy were not there and were not students of World War II. It is time for President Truman's critics to face reality and stop apologizing for the defeat of one of history's most brutal aggressors. At the same time, they should note that in the fifty years before Hiroshima, Japan started five wars; in the fifty years since, none.

The invasion of Japan (Operation Olympia) was scheduled for November, 1945. The 63rd Bomb Squadron had received its tentative assignment for the invasion; however, the actual targets had not been assigned. We were to bomb the beach head, return to Ie Shima, and re-arm for a second attack on the beach head. After returning from the second mission, plywood benches were to be installed in our bomb bays for paratroopers who would be dropped through the camera hatch. The paratroopers did not want to jump through a camera hatch at speeds above 115 miles per hour. A combat-loaded B-24 stalled at speeds slightly below 115 miles per hour. To make matters worse, we would be flying formation at night with another B-24 that was painted black and without running lights. I was one of many who was glad President Truman ordered the atomic bombs dropped.

I hate to think what would have happened in the United States if the Japanese had won World War II. Based on their actions in other places they conquered, it would have been pretty grim. That possibility was there, as the Japanese, with the help of the Germans, were working on an atomic bomb. They would never have hesitated to use it on Americans.

Surrender of Japan

On August 15, 1945, Emperor Hirohito had a recording played to the Japanese people announcing that Japan had surrendered and that the war was over. After that the last Americans to die were sixteen captured B-29 crew members who were taken to a small patch of woods on the island of

Kyushu where they were stripped and beheaded, one by one. Three American ships were sunk, the U.S. submarine *Bonefish* (all aboard were drowned) and the destroyer *Callaghan* went down, and the destroyer escort *Underhill* was lost.

I did get to see one important bit of history. After Japan had agreed to "unconditional surrender," a Japanese delegation was sent to General McArthur's headquarters in Manila to arrange for the actual surrender. The delegation flew from Japan to Ie Shima, where they changed from Japanese Betty bombers to American C-54 transports for the flight to Manila. We gathered along the runway to watch and take pictures. We knew we were watching history in the making. There were two Bettys in formation; they had been painted white with green crosses on the sides and wings for identification. They were to be met by American B-25s to escort them to the landing runway; P-51s flew top cover. To impress the Japanese even more, an American infantryman was posted, with slung rifle, every three feet down both sides of the runway. The Japanese pilots must have been a little more than nervous. One overshot the runway and ran off the end. No damage was done to the Betty. The flight crew remained on Ie Shima with their planes while the delegation was in Manila. I did not talk to the Japanese crew, but those who did said the Japanese spoke perfect English and said they had bombed Ie Shima a couple of nights before.

On October 1, while preparations were being made for the occupation of Japan, I was sent out on a weather reconnaissance mission from Korea down the China coast to Shanghai. There was a front along the flight path almost to Shanghai. I was able to descend over Shanghai and see where we had been so many times at night. One night during the war, as we were going down the Whang Po River, we noticed lights were going by above us. That day I found out the lights were on tall buildings along the Shanghai Turning Basin and that we were below the tops of the buildings.

Returning Home

When the combat crews got word that the war was over, there was no celebration. Some of the noncombatants and support people celebrated because they would be going home. My thoughts were the same as most of the combat crews.

"Thank God it is over, and I survived the worst conflict the world has ever known."

I never really thought I would survive the war and be going home. During the flight to the target area and while in actual combat, I was never able to think so fast and so clearly. It has been very hard for me to think back and relive some of those experiences. But we should never forget. Those of us who fought World War II owe it to future generations so they might make the world safe from future aggressors. Our nation learned a vital lesson from this war: never weaken our defenses as we did after World War I. Today we have the strongest military complex the world has ever seen and we need to keep it that way.

After World War II, the Cold War, the Vietnam War, and close calls on the ground and in the air throughout all of my air force career, I know someone has been watching over me and taking care of me. The crew still kids me about my rabbit's foot, but I know it was God who was with me.

Before we could return to the States, it was necessary to get travel orders from 5th Air Force. The request for the orders had to go through channels. It was initiated at the 63rd Bomb Squadron, then went to the 43rd Bomb Group, then on to 5th Air Force. It was necessary for each command to approve the request after which the orders had to go back through channels in reverse order. Since most of the administrative personnel had been overseas for two to three years, they were the first to be rotated back to the States. I imagine all orders other than their own were given a low priority. The rest of the troops simply had to sit and wait. The problem of logistics trying to get thousands of troops home was tremendous as you can well imagine. The problems of what to do with all the equipment had to be handled. Some of it was going to be needed for the occupation of Japan but much of it was simply abandoned.

People were rotated home based on how long they had been overseas. The first to go home were the support people. All of the cooks rotated, so our gunners volunteered to cook. None had any experience, but it kept them from hard details. Experience was not too necessary. They went to the navy supply point for supplies. They were given fifty cases of beets. So we got beets three meals per day and if we were lucky they were warmed up. After great urging they learned how to work the stove. I asked Pat Dowling what he knew about cooking and he said, "Simple. Take a meat cleaver and open a can of beets." When the fifty cases of beets were gone, they went back to the supply point and this time, the navy unloaded thirty more cases of beets. Fortunately, I started home before all the beets were gone this time.

Japanese peace delegation landing on Ie Shima en route to Manila to arrange the official surrender of Japan. The final papers of the official surrender were signed on the Battleship Missouri in Tokyo Bay, September 2, 1945.

The Japanese peace delegation.

All of our planes were ferried to Clark Field to be used to transport people back to the States. We were ordered to fly one of the squadron B-24s to Clark. We were told we would only be on the ground a couple of hours. A B-24 would pick us up and take us back to Ie Shima. I had been in the army long enough to know how they screwed things up, so I took my mess kit and shaving kit. I was about the only one who did. The B-24 did not show up, of course, and the depot at Clark would not accept our airplane because they claimed it was "war weary" or worn out. It would take too much maintenance to get it ready to fly back to the States where it would be junked anyway. We ate and shaved in shifts with everyone using my mess kit and shaving kit. We got some help from the Red Cross but little from the army. After five days we finally got in touch with the squadron by radio, and asked for instructions. They forgot to send the B-24. We were told to fly our aircraft on to Biak where it would be junked, and they would have a B-24 pick us up at Biak. Because of the condition of the aircraft we made relatively short flights landing at Peleliu and Morotai en route to Biak. I guess they were in fear of bodily harm because another war weary B-24 showed up at Biak. We did not get back to Ie Shima until September 13, 1945, almost a month after the war was over.

We waited around Ie Shima until November 9, almost two months after our last mission, when I received orders to return to the States. We were told, "The United States is east of here. Go home." This is where the crew broke up. Lt. Bob Burns, the bombardier, and I left together. We were given a ride in a B-24 to Yontan Air Base on Okinawa where we checked into an air transportation unit for a flight to Manila. This was good for a three- or four-day wait.

Fortunately, I recognized the lieutenant in charge of the dispatchers. I knew him from preflight and had seen him in a Red Cross tent on our first ferry mission to Ie Shima. I said, "Hi buddy. How're you doing?" He did not know me from a load of hay, but did not want to admit it, and he got us out on the next plane in a couple of hours. The flight took us to Nichols Field outside of Manila where we checked into a replacement center to wait for a troop ship. While in the depot, I heard the song, "Sentimental Journey" for the first time. It really had meaning for me. It did for a lot of people about that time. While I was in Manila, I weighed in at 125 pounds fully dressed. Before I left the States, I weighed 200 pounds stripped. I had lost more than 75 pounds during the tour in the Pacific.

After about ten days in Manila, I boarded the navy troopship, the *Admiral Mayo,* for passage back to the States. The trip was uneventful except for the time I was walking along the deck after dark, and suddenly found myself head over heels on the deck below, unaccustomed as I was to navy vessels. After all of the beets, the food on the ship was great. A navy lieutenant gave some of the officers aboard a tour of the ship. He complained that the ice cream did not seem as good as usual that trip. It must have been a tough war for some. We had not seen that kind of food in nearly a year.

The trip took about seventeen days. We passed under the Golden Gate Bridge and entered the San Francisco Bay and as we passed under the Bay Bridge, we were surrounded by fire boats spraying their fire hoses into the air; all of their ship's horns were blowing at the same time. On the side of a hill was a big sign saying "Welcome Home." Motor boats were circling the ship and a barge pulled along side with a band playing "Auld Lang Syne." It was a very exciting time for all of us who were eager to get home. When we landed, the Red Cross ladies had coffee and donuts waiting. It made me feel like everyone really cared about what I had done and been through. It was good to be home. It was a lot different from coming home from the Vietnam War when no one gave a damn.

I arrived in San Francisco on December 5, 1945, and from there was taken to Camp Stoneman by ferry. It was necessary to carry our own bag to the ferry and on to Camp Stoneman. I would not mention this except that I remember I was so weak that I could hardly lift it. When I reached Camp Stoneman, I saw a large number of telephone booths that had been provided for the service men returning home to call home free of charge. I called home and talked to Mother, Pap (my father), and Eva. I told them I would be taking a train to Fort Sam Houston in San Antonio. Eva told me that Peg and Bill Banister were married in October and were living in San Antonio, and I was to call them when I arrived.

The next day I had to go to the base exchange and buy a winter uniform. The clothes I had with me were all summer clothes and ready to be thrown out, which they were. When I arrived at Fort Sam, as we got off the train, a sergeant made an announcement: "Those who wish to get out of the service, get into the line for mustering out. Those who wish to stay in the service, get into the other line."

I didn't get in either line. Finally the sergeant came up to me and asked me what I wanted to do. I told him I had no intention of making that decision at that time. He said in a threatening manner, "Do you want to go see the lieutenant?"

I said, "Yeah, let's go see the lieutenant." When I told the lieutenant that I had no intention of making such a decision at that time, he said, "OK, come back tomorrow or the next day."

I called the Banister's, they gave me their address and I took a cab to their apartment. Eva was there to meet me. We spent the night there and the next day I went back out to Fort Sam to finish processing. I had not been paid in about six months. When I got paid, I had more money than I had seen at one time in my life. It left me with the feeling that being in the U.S. Air Corps was a pretty good idea. The other alternative was to get out of the service and go back to college using the GI bill and get my degree in aeronautical engineering. I had always wanted a military career and the idea of becoming an engineer and working for an aircraft company was not nearly so inviting. After all the war was over and the future of the aircraft industry might be such that engineers were not in great demand. So, I told the lieutenant I wanted to stay in. I had a 45-day leave coming, so Eva and I caught the train the next day to Houston.

The station in Houston was crowded with homecoming service men. We got off the train and spotted Mother and Pap right away. They did not see us as we walked up behind them. I will never forget when my mother turned around and saw me and threw her arms around me and gave me a big hug. I was facing the train and there was a woman on the train looking out the window. She saw us and knew that I had just gotten home from the war and she smiled and tears came running down her face. I wondered if she had lost someone in the war. It was good to be home again.

chapter 6

Training Command

AFTER A 45-DAY LEAVE, I reported back to Ft. Sam Houston in San Antonio in January, 1946. When I returned from overseas, having elected to remain in the service, I did not realize how difficult it would be to stay on active duty, as thousands of officers, especially pilots, also elected to stay in. There were far more than the needs of the peace time army air corps. Every one who wanted to stay was allowed to do so, but not for long. With all of the confusion at the end of the war, in 1946 only the planners in Washington knew what the manpower requirements would be for the peace time military services. The new separate air force was in the planning stage. In the meantime business had to go on as normally as possible and everyone was trying to make the best of it.

From Ft. Sam I was transferred to Mather Field in Sacramento, California. This was a pool of officers being assigned to the Training Command. A few people were released from active duty. I was not too involved, as I only spent two weeks there. Most of that time was spent in the hospital trying to cure the "jungle rot" (a bad case of athlete's foot) that I had picked up in the Pacific, caused by wearing wet, muddy boots too long. The ulcers on my toes had become infected and I was told they might have to come off. When I received my travel orders, they had not completely healed. When I got to Lowry Army Air Field in Denver, Colorado, in March, 1946, I checked in with the flight surgeon. He gave me some medicine to put on my feet that made me cry when I used it, it stung so badly. In fact it ate the metal top off the bottle, but it did the job.

Lowry and Buckley

There was nothing to do at Lowry. All of the jobs on the base had been filled many times over. To keep us busy, they sent us to a school, which was absolutely worthless. It was mostly a bull session that was taught by the chaplain's wife. Her main topic was "Life in the service before WWII." You can imagine how this went over with the pilots, most of whom had just returned from combat. Most of the students walked out, but I stayed. They were all released from active duty, but I got an assignment.

Eva joined me and we set up housekeeping for the first time. We found a basement apartment that was fully furnished in a new house. We had lots of room and the landlady and Eva became good friends. It was the nicest place we had so far. We had no car and I rode the street car to work. You could not buy a lot of manufactured items including cars and household items in those days because the factories were re-tooling after making war materials. But at last, we were on our way to building a future.

I became manpower control officer at Buckley Army Air Field, a satellite of Lowry Army Air Field on the edge of Denver, Colorado. To this day I am not sure what a manpower control officer is supposed to do. We were still receiving draftees or people in a "pipeline." They were to be sent to schools, mostly heavy equipment schools. There was no mission and none of these kids wanted to learn anything. It kept me and the senior noncommissioned officers (NCO) busy keeping them looking like they were working.

I was also responsible for making promotions below sergeant. There were not any promotions above that as all officers and NCOs were frozen in rank. Almost by accident I learned one non-flying regulation—that a person could be promoted from private to corporal without going through private first class (PFC). Buckley Field is where I began to realize that if a person was in the Reserve and did not have a job or a godfather, his days were numbered. There was still a great overage of officers, especially flying personnel.

Every year on April 21, Texans celebrate the battle of San Jacinto, when Texas won its independence from Mexico in 1836, and became a republic. Aggies all over the world get together for a Muster ceremony wherever they are. In 1946, General Eisenhower was to be the principal speaker at the Muster at College Station. A number of VIPs were scheduled to attend. The deputy base commander at Lowry was an Aggie, but could not attend, so it was easy to talk him into giving me a B-25 to fly a group of local Aggies down to College Station for the Muster.

When we got to A&M, I flew over the campus at a very low altitude a couple of times before we landed at Easterwood Field at College Station. When we got out of the plane, I was surprised to see a staff car with the commandant, who was a colonel, standing by it. When I went over and saluted him, he saw my first lieutenant's bars, turned around without returning my salute, and said, "Oh, shit!" He then got in the staff car and drove off, leaving me standing there. It was not until later that I found out why. Because there were no radio communications at Easterwood Field, buzzing the campus was the signal for the arrival of General Eisenhower and his staff.

Buckley was being closed or reverted back to the Reserve or National Guard, so all active duty people were being transferred. It became obvious at that time, in order to stay on active duty, it would be necessary to have more than just a pair of pilot's wings. Base personnel received a request for pilots to attend a school for weather officers, so I applied. I did not hear anything about the school and in the meantime, I received orders to Geiger Army Air Field, Spokane, Washington. I later found out that my application had been approved, but it was too late. I had already departed for my new assignment.

Geiger Army Air Field

We bought a second-hand 1940 Pontiac and drove to my new assignment at Geiger. It was August, 1946. Again after about three weeks searching, we found a furnished apartment in a farm house near Geiger Field, which belonged to a retired federal marshall.

Geiger was a part of the Air Training Command with a mission of training airmen in fields that were necessary for normal base operations, such as carpenters, plumbers, electricians, painters, etc. When I arrived at Geiger I was not too hopeful of getting a job, as I had been told most of the jobs on the base had been taken. The approval of my application to Weather Officer's School had not been forwarded to Geiger. While I was waiting in base personnel for an assignment, a colonel and a major were discussing the only non-flying regulation that I knew: whether a private could be promoted to corporal without going through PFC. Talk about luck! When I quoted the regulation, they thought I was well informed on administration and was just the person they wanted to fill the opening they had for the school secretary.

When I reported to a major who was to be my immediate superior, I was smart enough not to ask him what a school secretary does. He did not seem to be too happy with me because with my flight pay, I was being paid almost as much as he was. He commented that he was required by regulation to let me fly, but he expected me to be on duty from 8–5 five days a week. I would be free to fly after-duty hours and on weekends. With the unpredictable winter weather in Spokane, getting flying time was a real problem. We were afraid to leave the local area because we might be weathered out. More important, there was a regulation that pilots must get four hours or three hours and ten landings per month to maintain proficiency and to collect flight pay.

The base commander and the senior staff officers were all members of the Corps of Engineers. They ran the base like an army ground-force post. There was a great deal of animosity from the engineers because of the flight pay we received and they did not feel that we were real soldiers or necessary to their operation. Each Saturday there was a parade and they required the air force officers to march in among the enlisted men while their officers sat in the reviewing stand. That did not go over too well with the air force officers. We had not been required to do that since we were cadets.

When we flew the engineering officers on a cross-country flight, they treated us like their Jeep drivers. They would come up on the flight deck and order us around. By regulation they could have been ordered off the flight deck, but after we landed, we were back in their power and they knew it.

The reduction in force (RIF) was still in effect. The base continued to get quotas to release officers from active duty. Only the air force officers were released until there were only a few of us left. Later Training Command Headquarters found out what was going on, and a brigadier general made a surprise inspection. Many of the responsible commanders were either returned to the ground forces or were released from active duty.

I felt sure that I would be on the next reduction quota and was really sweating it out. One day a regular air force lieutenant colonel, William Miles, came into my office and announced he was my new boss and that the major who was my superior was working for him, too. More luck. He asked me if I knew where he could find an apartment. It just so happened that the one across the hall from ours was vacant.

He said, "Good, my wife is out in the car. Take her out to see it."

They moved into it and we became friends. He would not let them release me. He literally saved my career. The base staff had him transferred to base personnel because he was a registered engineer and outranked most of the staff. He took me with him. Had I continued working as the school secretary, my career in the air force would have been short.

I believe Lieutenant Colonel Miles must have manufactured a job for me. He made me responsible for applications to Officers' Candidate

School (OCS) and applications to pilot training. Both schools had been closed since the end of World War II. He also gave me the responsibility of screening enlisted men's hardship discharges and discharges of undesirable personnel. I did not let too many people out of the service on hardship discharges. I made applicants prove their hardship with receipts of their expenses. Most could not furnish them. Since the war was over, they were using hardship claims as a way to get out of the service. One day I received a call from the base commander telling me to get rid of all undesirables. I cleaned out the stockade and gave all of the prisoners a general discharge.

The sergeant major of the training battalion, a very sharp technical sergeant, had impressed me as being very proficient. When I was transferred to personnel to be in charge of OCS applications, I called him and told him that I thought he should apply for OCS. He said he was sorry, but he could not. A few days later he called me and asked if he could come and see me.

He said, "I can't apply because I am only seventeen years old, but I will be eighteen in a few months and would like very much to apply then." He then told me the following story.

He said that when he was thirteen years old, he enlisted in the army and while he was still thirteen, participated in the invasion of North Africa and was promoted to staff sergeant. After the invasion his age was discovered and he was shipped back to the States and given a minority discharge. He then proceeded to the nearest recruiting office where he re-enlisted; however, after a short period, the fact of his having been given a discharge was discovered, and he was again released from active duty. Not to be outdone, he went to another recruiting office and enlisted again, this time using his mother's maiden name.

I told him that I was obliged to report his age, but on second thought, I knew he would be back in the recruiting office again as soon as he was released. I decided to let him go, thinking that the army would be losing a good soldier.

One day I received orders to go to Peterson Field at Colorado Springs to pick up a B-25 and fly it back to Spokane. I was ferried down there in a B-26. When I got there, I had no trouble finding the airplane because it was the only one on the ramp. The base was closed. One of the engine's parts were strung out on the ground and stretched out clear to the wingtip. I asked the mechanic who was working on the plane, why the parts were strung out like that. He said, "I don't know anything about a B-25.

When I get ready to put it back together, I'll know which piece goes on next." I did not have a lot of faith in him.

The mechanic said it was not going be ready for a couple of days, so I told him how to get in touch with me at the Lowry Bachelor Officers' Quarters (BOQ), and to call me when it was ready and left. I got the pilot who flew me in to drop me off at Lowry Army Air Field in Denver so I would have a place to stay and see a few friends. I had to take all my flight equipment with me because I had no place to leave it.

During the night there was a snow storm in Denver and it was still snowing very heavily the next morning. I got a call from the mechanic telling me the plane was ready to go and the weather there was clear. I had a problem: How was I going to get to Peterson Field? The weather was below minimums in Denver, so I got a staff car from the motor pool to take me to town to catch a bus to Colorado Springs. Unfortunately, the staff car driver did not know there were two bus terminals in Denver and took me to the wrong one. They were several blocks apart and I had to walk to the other bus station. I was in my flying suit with a parachute slung over my shoulder, walking down the street in a snow storm. I drew quite a few chuckles on the way. When I got on the bus, the driver looked at me and said, "Lieutenant, we're not going that high. I really don't think you'll need that parachute."

One day we received a message from Training Command Headquarters at Randolph Army Air Field near San Antonio, Texas, stating that pilot training was going to reopen and that we were to appoint a board of pilots who were to screen applicants for pilot training. There were not too many pilots on the base, but we appointed enough to form a board. A Captain Lawrence E. (Johnny) Madsen was assigned to help me. The project was given a great deal of publicity and we had a large number of applicants. After all of the screening, we had twenty-five whom we felt were qualified.

We received a second message telling us to take all available applicants to Randolph. Johnny and I loaded all twenty-five into a C-47 to fly them to Randolph. A lot of the parents were there to see their sons off to pilot training. After we took off, Johnny asked me if I had the maps. I said, "No, didn't you get them?" It was a long way from Spokane to San Antonio, especially without maps. We felt we could not go back and let the parents know they had turned their sons over to a couple of idiots, so Johnny said, "If you can find the Grand Canyon, I can find San Antonio from there." I thought I could find the Grand Canyon so we proceeded from there. We recognized Austin from its street lights. At that time the street lights were bluish white. San Antonio was easy to find from there. When we landed, I went into Training Command Headquarters to report that we had the cadets. The officer in charge said, "Bring him in."

I said, "HIM! Hell, we've got twenty-five of them out there. You said bring all available." He said to bring them on in because some of the commands did not meet the request for applicants, and he would somehow make room for them. I wished them luck and told them, "I hope the next time I see you, you're Air Force pilots." We had been working on them for weeks getting them qualified. Training Command Headquarters kept half of them and sent the other half back to Geiger to wait for the next class. The army at Geiger did not know what to do with them. They were in cadet uniforms. They did not know whether to salute them or what.

If some of the things that happened at Geiger happened today, no one would believe it. One day while I was walking near the stockade, I saw a guard walking with a prisoner. They stopped and the guard handed his weapon to the prisoner while he tied his shoe. When the guard got his shoe tied, the prisoner gave back the weapon and they were on their way. Needless to say, I had a few words for the guard. They thought I was just another grouchy officer.

Another time when I was Officer of the Guard, I was checking the log book for special orders. I found an entry saying, "Don't sit on the bench in front of the guard house." I looked at the bench and it seemed ok to me, so I started looking in the log book for some reason not to sit on the bench. I found an entry made more than six months before saying, "Don't sit on the bench in front of the guard house because it has just been painted." The entry had been carried forward all that time. I made an entry as follows: "The paint is dry now. It's ok to sit on the bench." How we won World War II is a mystery. The Germans and Japanese could not possibly have been that screwed up.

The stockade at Geiger was next to the Airmen's Club. One Saturday night when I was Officer of the Guard, they were having a dance at the Airmen's Club. I received a call from the guard on the gate of the stockade. He stated that he needed my assistance. When I went to investigate, I found all of the prisoners were standing by the fence near the Airmen's Club. They were all stark naked. They thought it would be a good joke to embarrass the girls attending the dance. I told them to get into the barracks and they just stood there and laughed at me. I handed my side-arm to the guard on the gate and took his night stick and told a couple of the military policemen to follow me. When the prisoners saw us coming, they all ran into the barracks. I went into the barracks to try to make sure they did not come back out.

They had set a bucket of water above the door to fall on me when I opened the door. Fortunately, it did not work. When I got inside, I found all the prisoners sitting on their bunks still naked waiting for the bucket of water to fall on me. I told them to turn out the lights. They all turned them out except in the cell nearest the door. I reached up and turned the light off, but when I turned around to leave, the light came back on. The three prisoners in that cell were innocently sitting on their bunks enjoying their joke. I turned the light out again and turned to leave. The light came back on a second time. I turned the light back off and told them that if the light came back on again, I would put them in solitary confinement and not tell anybody where they were. It might take two or three days to find them. That got their attention and the light did not come back on.

We never had any trouble making new friends when we moved to a new base. The people were from all over the country and were making new homes for themselves just as we were. Still, it is always good to run into somebody from home. Spokane is a long way from Houston and we were going to spend our first Christmas away from home. We were delighted when we got a call from Suzie Banister, Bill's sister. I had known her for a number of years. She and her husband, Hobart Rowley, moved to Spokane from his home in Tacoma, Washington. He was with an insurance company. He had been a lieutenant in the field artillery during the war. We spent time together on the weekends teaching Eva and Suzie how to play bridge. She and Eva were pregnant at the same time and compared notes.

Shortly after we took the cadets down to Randolph, a quota came in for six four-engine pilots for assignment to Barksdale Army Air Field in Shreveport, Louisiana. I was hoping it was for the new B-36 that was just coming into the inventory. Johnny Madsen had flown the B-17 in England during the war, so I put Johnny and myself and a couple of friends on the list and we were soon gone.

On April 18, 1947, we drove away from Spokane. It was one of my happiest days. I had survived my ordeal with the Corps of Engineers. Thanks to Lieutenant Colonel Miles, I was headed back to a flying job. We had everything we owned packed into our 1940 Pontiac. Eva was due to have our first child in May, so we took it easy on the trip. We made Boise, Idaho, the first day and spent a couple of days resting and visiting friends and relatives. Our World War II bombardier, Bob Burns, had married a Boise girl he met when we went through B-24 training at Gowen Field and had moved to Boise. We were able to spend some time with my aunt Alida and her son, Wanek Stein, and his family.

Our next stop was Rock Springs, Wyoming, where my mother was visiting her family. We spent a couple of days visiting and then went on to Houston. My mother joined us for the trip home. The rest of the trip was uneventful.

When we got to Houston, we walked in on Eva's parents. They did not know we were coming. Eva had not told them because she knew they would worry about her making the long trip in her condition.

Barksdale Army Air Force Base

I stayed in Houston as long as I could waiting for the baby, who was due May 16, 1947. When he did not arrive, I had to go to Shreveport alone. When I checked into Barksdale Army Air Field, I was told to report to Col. Gabriel Disosway, who later became a general. When I went into his office, he had his feet on his desk, his hat over his eyes, and his arms folded across his chest. I thought he was asleep. I did not know what to do. I waited a few seconds, which seemed like hours, waiting for some acknowledgment. Finally I saluted. He returned my salute and said, "What the hell do you want?" I told him I was told to report to him for a flying assignment. He asked me how much B-17 flying time I had. When I told him none, that I didn't even know how to get in one, he replied, "A hell of a lot of good you are going to do me."

By then this poor first lieutenant was completely beat. I had not been talked to like that since I was a freshman at Texas A&M, and especially by a colonel. He then asked me how much four-engine flying time I had. When I told him I had about 800 hours in a B-24, he calmed down a little. He gave me one month to learn how to get in a B-17, learn to fly it, and get 100 hours in it. I was going to be a flight instructor in the first class. He then explained that advanced pilot training was being reopened. It had been closed since World War II. The first class was to begin in thirty days. When he finished, he asked if I had any questions.

I said, "Yes sir, can I have a leave?"

He said, "Christ no, didn't you hear anything I just said?"

I must have looked pretty dejected because he asked me why I wanted the leave. When I told him my wife was expecting our first baby at any

Boeing B-17G, Flying Fortress, used for pilot training after World War II.

time, he put his arm around my shoulder and walked me to the door and said, "Well, you'd better be there." He told his secretary to give me ten days leave, then turned to me and said, "When you get back, I'm going to fly your ass off because you are going to get that 100 hours and learn to fly a B-17 before the first class starts."

When I returned from leave, still without the new baby, I met Colonel Disosway's demands and instructed in B-17s for two years. The checkout program was pretty much of a self-help program. Some of the pilots who had flown B-17s before gave a couple of instruction rides to those who had not flown them before but had experience in the B-24s and the four-engine C-54s. From then on we were on our own.

One day I was flying with Capt. John Irby, who had flown the C-54, but did not know any more than I did about the B-17. We decided to try testing the plane to see how it would fly by cutting an engine. After we tried that, I said, "John, I wonder how this plane would fly on two engines." He said, "I don't know, let's find out." I cut number three and four engines and he cut numbers one and two ignitions. It sure got quiet. From then on it was not three people including John and myself and the flight engineer trying to start the engines, it was all six hands going at once.

Pilot training after World War II consisted of six months in basic training at Randolph Army Air Field where cadets would learn to fly T-6s, a single-engine trainer. The multi-engine students were also to receive six months training in advanced flight training. There was no "Primary" as we knew it. As an experiment, the multi-engine students were divided in half. One half were to receive their training in B-25s and the other half in B-17s. The experiment of taking students directly from T-6s into B-17s worked fine, but it got too expensive and we converted to B-25s. It seemed a little ridiculous to me that they were still cutting pilots, and at the same time, training new ones. The argument was that there was a need for younger people for the future. Most of the students were World War II navigators and bombardiers upgrading to pilots.

When Johnny Madsen and I walked in to meet the first class of cadets, there sat the same cadets we had recruited from Washington. They had been through basic and were now ready for advanced. When they saw us, they said, "Oh God," all in one voice.

On July 4, I was able to get a little time off, so I drove to Houston to bring Eva and the new baby back to Shreveport. None of our group had enough rank to get quarters on base. We were on our own to find some place to live in Shreveport or Bossier City. Before I picked up Eva, I rented a garage apartment that had been listed at base housing. It had been an old servants' quarters that had been renovated somewhat. It had five rooms: a kitchen, bedroom, dining room, living room, and bath. It had an outside staircase that led up to a porch, which had been converted into a "living room." It was no wider than the staircase. I could sit on the couch on one side of the room and put my feet in the window across the room. In those days people had never heard of air conditioning or insulation and that place was really hot in the summer. We bought a window fan and the breeze helped some. There was one advantage to the apartment. After the floor had been swept, it was not necessary to pick up the dirt. It had fallen through the cracks into the garage below.

We did not have much money, so our interior decorating was somewhat meager to say the least. We bought an old stove and refrigerator. You could not buy anything new yet because the factories still had not caught up with the post-war demand. We got some paper curtains, the newest thing out. They were fine except there was a puddle of water on the floor beneath them due to the humidity. We only lived there about three months when we moved into a new two-bedroom house. The house was nice but it was several miles through Shreveport traffic to Barksdale.

Flight instructors at Barksdale Air Force Base, 1948. Standing, left to right: John Irby, Art Lattimer, Bill Lonsdale, Al Stein, Pete Peterson, and Fuzzy Fussell. Kneeling, left to right: Lieutenant Thompson, Unknown, Bruce Pope, and Russ Kline.

Moving was never a problem. We got a case of beer, drew a truck from the base motor pool, and let our friends know we were moving. Our friends helped us and we would be moved in a short time. Of course, we did the same for them. None of us had a lot of furniture that we were afraid would get damaged. Finally a new duplex housing project opened right next to Barksdale, so we put our name on the waiting list and four months later moved into a one-bedroom duplex as soon as it was available. A couple of months later our name came up on the list for a two-bedroom and we moved again. All of our close friends lived in the general area and we were never lonesome.

These were some of my most pleasant years in the air force. All of the instructors were young captains or first lieutenants. Most had been married a short time and were starting their families. We were all very close friends and Eva and I fit right into the group. I was getting all the flying time I wanted. We worked hard and we played hard. Our entertainment center was the Barksdale Officers' Club. We had many memorable parties there.

The Flying Training Command was headquartered at Barksdale Army Air Field. It was commanded by a World War I pilot, John Cannon, who was now a four-star general waiting for retirement. Needless to say no one ever called him "Uncle John" to his face. He had a personal B-17 that had been plushed up and he named it *The Canon Ball*. On the side of the plane, under the pilot's side window, was a big red circle with *The Canon Ball* painted beneath it. He had flags painted, representing all the many countries in which he had served, below that.

One day I was in the traffic pattern at Barksdale teaching my students how to land a B-17, when another B-17 cut in front of me so I could not land. Thinking it was just another instructor, I turned inside of him on

Flight instructors at Barksdale Air Force Base, 1949. Standing, left to right: Capt. Fuzzy Fussell; Lt. Nick Xenakis; Capt. Lawrence E. (Johnny) Madsen; Lt. Art Latimer; Lieutenant Thompson; Capt. G. B. Bell; Capt. Jay Harralson; Lt. Allan Stein; Major McMahan; Capt. Rud Morley, flight commander; Capt. Dale Neely; Lt. Bill Eaton; Capt. Robert Kensey; Capt. Paul M. Montag; Sergeant Layseth; and Sergeant Mangum. Kneeling, left to right: Maj. R. P. (Dick) Haney, flight commander; Capt. Tommy Mills; Capt. Bob Paulin; Capt. Russ Kline; Lt. Col. Kelly Mitchem, director of four-engine flying; Lt. Salvador Danna; Lt. Bill Clay; Major McCorry, flight commander; Lt. Mac Roberts; Capt. John Irby; and Capt. Robert Lecates.

the base leg so he could not land either. Just as I was committed to my turn, I looked at the other B-17 and it was *The Canon Ball* and Uncle John was flying it. He called the tower yelling, "Get his number! Get his number!" and he was yelling for me to "Stop! Stop!" My only thoughts were to escape. I did not give my aircraft number to the control tower when I turned onto the base leg, which was normal procedure. I added high cruise power to my plane and headed south as fast as it would go. He chased me for about twenty minutes, but I out-ran him. My B-17 was lighter than his. My students thought it was very funny. I told them if they wanted to achieve their dream of silver wings, they would keep their big mouths shut. Uncle John made a big issue about the incident after he got on the ground, but none of my students told what happened. Uncle John retired soon and I was safe. In the air force you have never really lived until you have cut a four-star general out of the traffic pattern.

One day a navy pilot landed a carrier plane at Barksdale. After he turned off the runway, he folded the plane's wings and taxied into *The Canon Ball*. This may be normal navy procedure, but most people thought he was just showing off. I am sure running into *The Canon Ball* is not normal navy procedure. One of my friends happened to go by Uncle John's office. The door was open and Uncle John had that poor navy pilot at a very stiff brace and was giving him hell. He threatened him with bodily harm if he ever landed at Barksdale again.

At one of our many parties at the Officers' Club, Eva and I were dancing when Eva saw Uncle John. She had never seen him before and seeing anyone with white hair on an Air Base in those days was very unusual. She asked me, "Who is that old man?"

"What?" I said. I could not hear her over the music. So she repeated it, only this time, the band stopped and there was dead silence and everyone on the dance floor heard her including Uncle John, who was standing right behind her. I hoped he looked around wondering who said it and hoped he remembered that one day, he was a young lieutenant.

Grave Registration Duty

The summer of 1948, I was picked for six weeks temporary duty to Grave Registration. This was a program whereby the United States brought back to the families the men who had been killed and buried in foreign countries during World War II. The bodies were brought by boat to New York and San Francisco and from there, loaded on special trains equipped for the purpose, and sent to local areas for distribution to their home towns and families. The ones for the south central area were sent to the 8th Army Mortuary near Fort Worth. When the bodies reached the mortuary, they were unloaded, the caskets checked for damages from shipping and for odors. Repairs were made, or if necessary, they received a new casket. They then went into another section of the mortuary where they awaited being escorted to their homes. Each body was escorted home by a member of the armed forces who was of the same branch of the service, same race, rank, and religion as the deceased. The bodies were taken to the local mortuaries in flag-draped caskets and if the family requested a military funeral, we would assist in any way we could, which included presenting the flag to the next of kin. I found this difficult. One could not help but feel some of the grief these families were suffering.

When I walked into the shipping section of the mortuary for the first time to escort a body home, I was shocked to see the huge number of flag-draped caskets stretching almost as far as the eye could see. It was a sobering sight.

I escorted one young lieutenant to Oklahoma City. The mortuary picked up the body from the train, and I went to inform his mother we had arrived. She was a waitress in a restaurant and when she saw me in my uniform, she came running to me with her arms out and stopped about five feet from me and began to cry. She thought for a moment that I was her son.

Another lieutenant and I escorted two brothers home to Goodnight, Texas. We had to take them to Clarendon because Goodnight did not have a mortuary. The two boys were apparently very popular and well-known in the area and I guess were high school football heroes. We pulled the caskets up to the door of the baggage car and left the door open. As we passed through these small towns, we stood at attention at the heads of the caskets. It was amazing to see the crowds of people who came down to the stations of these little towns to watch as we passed through. We got off at Clarendon, and the caskets were loaded into hearses. There was a parade through the downtown district of Clarendon with people lining the streets. Many were crying. All the businesses were closed for the parade. Those were sad days for many families all over the country.

The father was very upset with the army and me in particular. He seemed to blame me for the death of his sons because I represented the army. He wanted to open the caskets to make sure they were indeed his sons. The mortician, who had a record of the condition of the remains, came to me and said, "If he opens that casket, it will be the saddest day of his life"—not because his sons were not in the caskets, but because the bodies were in very bad condition. I asked the father if he remembered his sons' dog tags (identification tags). The father said, "Yes."

I went to the head of one of the caskets, got the son's tag, pulled it off, and handed it to him. That seemed to satisfy him. The army was very meticulous about identification. As a matter of fact, when the army exhumed the bodies, they made sure that they only had one above the ground at any one time.

The night before the funeral, men from the local chapter of the Veterans of Foreign Wars and American Legion post met in a local parking lot to practice the procedure for a military funeral. To get away from the sorrows of the family, the other lieutenant and I watched them. Before we were sent out on escort duty, we received instructions as to how to conduct a military funeral, but were instructed not to interfere with local funeral arrangements.

When the practice started, everyone was very congenial, but soon they began to argue about the correct procedures. Each one had his own idea of how it should be done and before we knew it, they were about to come to blows. They finally asked us to help, which we did and it all ran smoothly after that. Everyone seemed satisfied.

I escorted a body to San Antonio to be buried in the National Cemetery at Fort Sam Houston. I was met by civilian representatives of the local funeral home and I rode to the funeral home with them. When all the paperwork was completed, the mortician asked me if I had made arrangements for a place to stay until the funeral. When I told him I had not, he said they had an extra room and I was welcome to stay there. They then asked me if I would like to see what happens to a person when they drive too fast. We went to the embalming room where a body of a man lay on one of the tables. They pulled the sheet back and exposed his face. He had lost half of his face in an automobile accident. They were very proud of the reconstruction they had done on his face. It had been built up with wax, a towel had been pressed into the wax to give it texture, and graphite had been rubbed into the wax to make it look like the other side of his face. I had seen more than I wanted to see. The room they gave me to sleep in was called a "slumber room" where bodies were laid for viewing by the families and friends of the deceased. I believe they were trying to spook me. It did not keep me awake. I slept soundly.

The next morning I rode to the cemetery in the hearse carrying the body. The deceased's family was already there seated in chairs by the grave site. The military burial party was about twenty minutes late to take the casket out of the hearse and carry it to the grave site. There was another thirty-minute wait for the chaplain to arrive. This was a very stressful period for the next of kin. When the volley was fired, I thought the deceased's mother was going to faint. Further, when the burial party bent over to fold the flag to be presented to the mother, you could see one of the them was wearing light blue socks. It is always a difficult time for all when the flag is presented to the next of kin. I thought it could have been handled better. I let my feeling be known to the burial party and the chaplain.

It is a very difficult time for the family of the deceased and also difficult for the escort. What do you say to the mother who has lost her son in combat when the flag is presented? Words may come to mind, but never seem adequate to the moment.

Most of the experiences of the escorts were sad as to be expected. However, some were amusing and even adventuresome. We all compared notes when we returned and there were some good stories to come out of it.

One escort took a body to a small town that had turned out in full for the funeral. The grieving widow, mother, father, and five-year-old son were sitting in the front row. The chapel service went well; however, at the graveside services when the firing party fired the volley, it was too much for the grandmother and she fainted. The little boy jumped up on the mound of dirt and said, "Hold everything! Some son-of-a-bitch just shot Gramma!"

Another escort was gone for about two weeks and was considered absent without leave (AWOL). When he returned, he told this story.

The train stopped at a desolate spot in New Mexico. The casket was unloaded and he got off with it. The train continued on and left him there. There was not a soul in sight. Since there was no place to sit down, he sat on the casket and waited for a couple of hours wondering what to do. Finally an old Indian came along with a wagon. With much difficulty the two of them loaded the casket onto the wagon and proceeded to the tribal campground. When they arrived, the people insisted the casket be opened. They gathered around to watch. Fortunately they recognized the deceased, and the escort was made an honorary member of the tribe. They insisted that he remain for their ceremony, which involved burning down the deceased's hogan. All of this took about ten days.

Another escort delivered a body to another small town in Texas' Rio Grande Valley. After the escort turned the body over to the mortuary, he went to the hotel and went to bed. After drinking much tequila, the mourners decided they were going to open the casket to see their old buddy. They opened it, and fortunately recognized him, but they could not get the casket closed. They did not want to wake the mortician so they went to the hotel to get the escort up and rousted him öut in the middle of the night. The next day there was to be a Catholic funeral. The mourners, still somewhat under the influence, insisted that the escort replace the priest in leading the procession from the church to the cemetery swinging an incense pot. The escort never said so, but I will bet after he was rousted out in the middle of the night, he also helped the mourners with a little of the tequila.

One thing that impressed me most about this duty was that all of their loved ones had held out hope that the government had made a mistake. That their sons were somehow still alive and perhaps in a hospital somewhere unconscious and misidentified, and one day they would be coming home. When their bodies were finally back home, they could then begin to deal with their loss and know for sure that they were indeed gone. I was also impressed with the way our government handled the whole program. I was very proud to have been a part of it.

The U.S. Air Force

On June 29, 1948, while I was still on Grave Registration duty, I received an urgent message telling me that I must return to Barksdale before July 1 to determine my status in the new U.S. Air Force. I was given the option of transferring as a first lieutenant into the new air force or staying in the army as a reserve captain on inactive status. Naturally I went with the new air force. There was no immediate change, except for our aircraft call signs. We were now, air force instead of army. We all had begun to look rather shabby. Our old pink and green army officer's uniforms were worn out. We knew we would be going into new air force blue uniforms, and no one wanted to spend money on new army uniforms.

Money was still a problem for the service. Congress was still trying to pay for World War II, and "who needs a military service since we will never have another war?" As always during peace time, the military is a useless burden on the tax payers, but during war time, nothing is too good for the boys in blue.

In 1948, two months before the end of the fiscal year, we ran out of aircraft fuel and had no money to buy more. There was not any flying until we could get more money from Congress. The RIF was still in effect, but now it was making a little more sense as the cuts were now based on performance and ability. The air force wanted to keep cutting the service, so those officers who were cut were offered a rating of master sergeant if they would stay on active duty, which many did in hopes of getting their commissions back in the future. Needless to say, this killed the few enlisted promotions there were for the troops. After a few months the effect became obvious and the offer was reduced to staff sergeant.

The B-17 had been replaced as an active bomber by the B-29 and B-36. It was too expensive to continue using the B-17 as a trainer for student pilots. In late 1948, we ferried all of the B-17s out to a depot where they were given to the Chinese or used for air rescue. They were replaced by B-25s that had all of the turrets and armament removed. They had been in storage since World War II and were in terrible shape. We got a lot of practice flying on one engine. Maintenance finally got all of the B-25s in good condition and we received our checkouts locally. Of all the aircraft I flew in the air force, the B-25 was my favorite. It was easy to fly, faster and better constructed than either the B-24 or the B-17. However, it had straight exhaust stacks and was very noisy. All of the instructors ended up with hearing waivers.

The people who were released from active duty all had jobs on base. It was up to those who remained to take over those jobs as additional duties. In addition to being a B-25 flight instructor, I instructed B-25 engineering in ground school. I also was in charge of a technical supply for the mechanics and was an assistant to the air installations officer who was in charge of all of the buildings on Barksdale. Needless to say, I did not get too much time off, but I was still on active duty. That was the most important thing.

One of my jobs with air installations was to increase building maintenance to justify the money spent on labor. All of the maintenance employees were civilians and were not too cooperative. One of the hangars had a leak in the roof and four maintenance men were dispatched to repair it. The repair crew had been gone for several hours when the major in charge of air installations asked me to check on the progress of the roof repair. I climbed up on the hangar roof and found all of the men asleep. No one was trying to locate or repair the leak. I ordered them off the roof and reported what I had found to the air installations officer. He tried to fire the men, but they appealed to their local congressmen and were returned to work. The major was relieved of command and my services were no longer needed. I was beginning to learn about government bureaucracy.

When I took over the technical supply, an inventory had to be taken and we found they were short many small hand tools, pliers, screw drivers, and such. No one knew what happened to them, but we suspected they were taken home by the mechanics. These shortages had to be accounted for on paper and it was up to me to come up with them. One of the sergeants told me that after World War II, there was no accountability. As a matter of fact, there was a great overage. All surplus tools were dumped into a lake on the far side of the base. I sent a couple of the clerks out to the lake where they dove and recovered many of these tools. Of course, they were in bad shape and were salvaged and returned to the lake, but it made up for the shortage, or at least part of it. We made screw drivers out of welding rods, which passed for tools without handles and they too were salvaged. We found large items, such as B-17 tow bars that had simply been parked behind hangars and forgotten. It took a couple of months to clear it up, but we finally did. On top of that some of my sergeants stole items from the salvage yard and then turned them back in for salvage. What a mess. This is no longer necessary. They have a certain limited amount of losses that can be written off.

The Berlin Airlift

When the Germans surrendered, the Russians controlled the land around city of Berlin; however, the control of Berlin was divided between the Russians, French, British, and Americans. This arrangement was decided at a treaty among the four nations at Yalta shortly before the war in Europe ended. The French, British, and Americans each had both air and ground corridors through Russian-held territory to reach their Berlin sectors. In June, 1948, in an attempt to gain control over all of Berlin, the Russians blocked all of the three western countries from using their corridors across Russian-held territory. The Russians did not think the United States, Great Britain, or France would consider the areas they controlled in Berlin worth fighting for and they would thus gain control over all of Berlin. For ground forces to push their way through the ground corridors may have started a war with Russia, so a decision was made not to abandon the people of Berlin and to supply minimum needs of Berlin's western sectors by air.

All C-47s within a reasonable distance of Germany were quickly assembled at airdromes near the Russian Sector. The planes were to be flown by local air force pilots. The flight movements soon required C-54 cargo aircraft and crews from all the air forces and navy to implement the program. A continuous flow of planes carrying supplies were flown into Tempelhof, Gatow, and Tegel Air Bases in Berlin. The operation became known as the "Berlin Airlift." The tempo of flights soon required replacement of the pilots. Requisitions for pilots were sent out through the air forces for replacements. The pilots were to be on temporary duty to the airlift for two to three months. It turned into one of the most astounding missions in history. Tons and tons of materials, coal, food, milk, and medical supplies kept the Berliners supplied with necessities. It was a mission of mercy for our former enemies and cemented relations between the Allies and Germany.

When my training squadron received a request for a pilot, I volunteered because I thought it would make my position more secure and for a period, I would be immune from the release of reserve officers. Also it would look good on my records and perhaps further my career. Another pilot also volunteered for the same request. Our commander had us match coins; the winner would go immediately and the loser would go on the next quota. I lost. The Russians finally were convinced by May, 1949, that we were determined to supply Berlin by air and they opened the ground corridors. So I did not get to go.

Missing B-17

On July 4, 1948, I was airdrome officer (AO). It was a very quiet night and nothing was going on. I received a call from a tower operator saying that an airplane flying by reported that a B-17 had crashed south of Barksdale and was burning. I asked him if any of our B-17s had taken off during the night and he said no. I checked with the operations dispatcher to see if any of our B-17 pilots had filed a clearance. He also said no. Then I called the Federal Aviation Administration (FAA) Flight Center, which controlled the movement of all aircraft in the area. I asked if there were any B-17s in the area. He said there was one and he had reported a B-17 crash south of Barksdale. So, where did this B-17 come from?

By this time the mechanics were beginning to report to duty to prepare the planes for the morning flights. I called our line chief in charge of all ground crews. I asked him if all our planes were here. He answered,

"Of course they're all here." I could tell he thought I must be a nut. I told him to go count them. In a few minutes he called back and said, "My God, Lieutenant, one of them is missing!"

With that I called our group commander, explained the situation, and suggested he have a head count to see who was missing. When I pressed the tower operators again, they admitted that it was a very quiet night because of the holiday and they may have dozed off a little. It turned out that the crew chief of the missing plane was also missing.

When the fire trucks returned from the crash site they confirmed it was indeed our B-17 and the crew chief was dead. On investigation it was found that a couple of our crew chiefs had consumed too much beer at the NCO Club and decided that if those dumb cadets could fly a B-17, they could, too. They went to their planes and were going to fly formation. One of them sobered up enough to realize that if he took off, he would either wind up in the stockade (jail) or the cemetery.

During the official investigation someone asked one of the firemen from the flight-line fire department if he had seen a B-17 starting its engines. He replied: "Yes."

They asked him why he did not do something about it. He replied: "What's so unusual about a B-17 starting its engines on an Air Force base?"

Flying Proficiency

It was not until I was transferred to the Flying Training Command at Barksdale that I felt that I became a proficient pilot. During our tour in the Pacific during World War II, our flying experience was greatly exaggerated because of the number of hours we flew. After I graduated from pilot training, I received very little opportunity for any additional flight training. Our training was as a crew and all of the other crew members needed training in their specialty.

During the war combat takeoffs were very critical because of our over-weight load of bombs and fuel. After reaching the cruise altitude, the auto pilot was engaged and remained so for most of the mission. Sometimes it was disengaged when we were actually attacking a target. During the long combat missions the auto pilot was a must. Two pilots would have been completely exhausted without it.

On the long seventeen- or eighteen-hour missions we made only one takeoff and one landing. I doubt that we made thirty-five landings from the time we left the states until the war was over. I personally made only four or perhaps six of the landings. We never practiced emergency procedures or flew instruments or practiced instrument approaches during the entire time we flew a B-24. We were an accident waiting to happen by today's standards. We were fortunate an emergency never occurred because I doubt if we could have handled it. We were no different from any of the other crews or servicemen who were sent into combat with very little training, which contributed to the high casualty rates.

In the training command I made as many as twenty to twenty-five landings a day until the students checked out or learned to land the B-17 or B-25. After they checked out, they seldom landed without a simulated emergency. The students became very proficient and so did I. It was impossible to compare it with World War II training.

Cadets today are much more mature. In order to get a commission in the air force today, cadets must first have a college degree and then apply for a commission, after which they must attend Officers' Training School. Only then can they be eligible for pilot training. The planes in the inventory of today's air forces are very expensive and are equipped with the latest technology. It is very expensive to train professional pilots, therefore cadets must commit themselves to an extended service period after graduation from pilot training.

In 1947, pilot training was reactivated to train pilots for the future air force. At the same time the Air Force Instrument School was activated at Barksdale to teach instrument flying to pilots. This training was sadly neglected during the war because the instructors were not qualified. Pilots were sent from all over the air force to Barksdale to take the course in instruments so they could then go back to their bases and train other pilots. In advance pilot training we taught the same curriculum as the instrument school. We were graduating much more proficient pilots than those who trained during the war.

When the weather was too bad for students to fly, the instructors would pair up and go looking for the worst weather they could find to fly through until one pair flew through a West Texas thunderstorm and ran into large size hail. When they landed the B-25, major repairs were required. The Wing commander put a stop to that.

After several years of demonstrating different instrument procedures and maneuvers, we became very proficient instrument pilots. Later when I was an instructor pilot and flight examiner in the Strategic Air Command (SAC), I expected the same proficiency. Unfortunately I did not always get it and failed a lot of pilots. It was my duty not to allow weak pilots to fly SAC aircraft with nuclear weapons on board.

It is vitally important for our country's leaders to realize the lessons we learned the hard way in World War II, especially with today's hi-tech aircraft. It takes many hours, even years, of training to turn out good pilots or any other military soldiers. We owe it to them to recognize this and have them ready for whatever they may have to face. After all, being second best in the air is unacceptable.

While I was at Barksdale, the FAA wanted a standard testing system to check airline pilots, so they asked for our help. A very comprehensive system was developed by the Air Force Instrument School. The FAA used air force advance pilot training instructors on which to test the new system. Several of us made six flights while being graded by FAA check pilots. In the end they liked the test and it became the standard for FAA check pilots. I was offered an air transport rating, which is required for airline pilots, but I had no desire to become an airline pilot. I wanted to stay in the air force.

When we received a new class into B-25 transition, the cadets had just completed their six months in T-6 basic training. I was assigned four students and as the training progressed, one of the students proved to be very weak. He worked very hard and was a very likable person and I tried very hard to keep him up with the class, but it was almost impossible. I should have eliminated him.

We used the El Dorado, Arkansas, municipal airport for takeoff and landing training. My weak student was at the controls one day when he lost control of the aircraft on a landing and ran off the side of the runway. I had to take control of the aircraft. When we stopped, we were in a foot of deep fresh mud. An air force fire truck arrived and they were about to tow it out, but I was afraid there had been damage to the nose wheel, so I went over to the truck and got a shovel. I handed it to the cadet and told him, "You put it in. You dig it out." After he dug it out far enough that it could be towed without damaging the B-25, I flew it back to Barksdale with the gear down because I was still afraid of damage to the gear. When we got back to Barksdale and landed, we caused quite a stir because the plane was covered with mud.

I should have used this incident to eliminate him, but he felt so bad about the incident, I thought he was going to cry. I felt sorry for him and let him graduate with his class. I hoped that when he went into a tactical unit, he would be given check rides and would eventually gain proficiency. I was wrong. About two months later he was killed. It was determined to be "pilot error." This was tough to take, but it made me determined to uphold pilot proficiency. Perhaps in the long run, it saved other borderline students.

That reminds me of another student who was flying when we were coming home one night from El Dorado. I told the cadet to take us home. There was a thunderstorm off to the right and I knew exactly what he would do. He used the radio compass to home in on Barksdale radio; however, the radio compass homed in on the thunderstorm. I thought, "I'm going to teach him a lesson," and I just let him go. Soon it was raining and I had instructed him before to turn on the landing lights to see if he was picking up wing ice when in this situation. He had not done so, so I asked him if it was raining. He said, "Yes, Sir." And I said, "How in hell do you know?"

He replied, "Because the windshield leaks and I'm all wet." All I could say was that it sure beat the hell out of looking out the window.

Flying with these young bright cadets was interesting to say the least. One of my best students was sent to Randolph Air Force Base as an instructor pilot in basic flight training when he graduated. I ran into him in Vietnam and he told me this story.

He was shooting landings with a cadet in a T-6. The student was on the final approach before landing, when he hit one rudder and the opposite aileron. This caused the T-6 to snap roll. They were upside down and headed for the runway. All the instructor could do was to keep it rolling. He said the plane touched down just as he got it right side up.

I asked him, "What did you do?"

He said, "I went home and changed my shorts."

chapter 7

Reese Air Force Base

IN THE SUMMER OF 1949, a B-36 landed at Barksdale and Gen. Curtis Lemay got out. The SAC had taken the base over for 2nd Air Force Headquarters. The Training Command had to pack up and move. My squadron moved to old Lubbock Army Air Field, which had been renamed Reese Air Force Base near Lubbock, Texas, where I received my wings in 1944. The field had been deactivated after the war and was loaned to Texas Tech University as a vet village for students on the GI Bill. The barracks were the same hastily constructed wooden buildings erected for the war effort. They were only supposed to last for seven years. Many of the barracks had been converted into apartments for married students. Physically it was in bad condition, but it was small, away from most air traffic, and more suited for flight training.

When we got our orders to move, we flew the B-25s to Reese. The wives stayed in Shreveport and packed. A C-47 was to pick us up the next day and take us back to Barksdale to be with the families for the move. Naturally the C-47 did not show up for a week. We slept in the BOQ that had been closed for about four years. We were provided with a cot and sheets. The Officers' Club had been used as a skating rink by the Texas Tech students and was in real bad shape. Someone found a couple of picnic tables and a grill, so we had hamburgers and beer three meals a day. Nobody complained because we did not have to work and had a good vacation.

Eva missed all this because the stork was due again and I had taken her to Houston to her parents on Labor Day, 1949. Bob put in his appearance on October 25, and I went down and picked them up on Thanksgiving weekend and took them to Lubbock. When Eva got to Lubbock, I had the furniture, etc. moved in. The house was not in a very good part of town, but it was brand new. The linoleum had not been put down in the kitchen, but it was a place to stay and we were glad to get it. We put our names on the list for a two-bedroom place nearer the base, but had to wait for it to be completed. With the help of some of our friends, Eva moved there in March while I was at Academic Instructors School at Craig Air Force Base near Selma, Alabama. It was a nice place and close to the other air force families, but it was small. We had to eat at the kitchen table and if the phone rang during a meal and was for me, I had to go out the back door and come in the front to answer it.

One morning the headlines in the Lubbock newspaper announced that the mayor had received a wild lion shipped directly from Africa. A very perplexed mayor claimed he had not ordered the lion and did not know how or why it was sent to him. It seems that one of the airmen with the same name from Reese Air Force Base had ordered the lion. He wanted to train it so he could join the circus and become a lion tamer. He made a lion cage in the base shop and painted it green and gold. He got a green and gold costume, boots, whip, and all.

The base commander came up with the idea that we should have a "county fair" to raise money to renovate the married enlisted men's quarters because the air force was too broke to do it. The airman and his lion were going to be the main attraction of the fair. Some of the airmen's buddies pushed the lion cage out on the flight line in front of the crowd. Oh, what a magnificent sight it was when he appeared in his green and gold lion-taming suit! After taking several bows, he climbed into the cage with the lion.

The airman was ready, but the lion had no desire to be tamed regardless of the green and gold suit. The lion gave him a working over you would not believe. If it had not been for some of his buddies beating the lion off with sticks, he would no doubt have been killed. Needless to say the airman spent some time in the base hospital. In the meantime his buddies pushed the lion cage to the edge of the base; however, a group of the wives who lived on the base went to the base commander and demanded that the lion be removed. There was a lot of joking at happy hour about turning the lion loose. The wives were afraid someone with too much to drink might actually turn the lion loose and they were afraid for their children. The base commander agreed and ordered the lion off the base.

The man who owned a filling station across the street from the main gate offered to let the airman put the lion next to his station. He thought people would come to see the lion and buy gas. There were not too many lions in Lubbock. The airman and his buddies pushed the lion's cage over to the gas station. The wives were still not too happy about having the lion that close. Sadly the problem was solved one night when someone shot and killed the lion.

That sounds like the end of the story but it is not. Years later when I was stationed at Maxwell Air Force Base in Montgomery, Alabama, a circus came to town. I took my little granddaughter, Susan. One of the acts was a lion-taming act. The lion tamer came out in a green and gold suit and on the back of his shirt was printed, "World Famous Lion Tamer" with the same name as the airman at Reese. I don't know if it was him, but it could have been. Some people just learn slowly.

One morning as we were reporting to work for the morning flight, our line chief, who was in charge of aircraft maintenance, came storming into operations mad as a hornet.

"What the hell did you guys do to one of my airplanes last night?" When we all denied any knowledge of wrong-doing, he yelled, "Come, look!"

We went out to the flight line and he showed us the damage on a T-6. The right aileron was hanging below the wing by the control cable; the flaring on the bottom of the right wing had long gashes in it; and the plane had a flat tire on the right main landing gear.

A cadet was scheduled to fly it the night before but, fortunately, never got airborne. He would have been killed if he had. The squadron commander went looking for him. He found him in ground school. When confronted, the cadet said he and another cadet had a bet to see who could get off the ground first. He was going to outsmart his friend by cutting across the center of the field to get ahead of him on take off. He missed the normal turn off from the ramp onto the taxiway and thought he was taking a short cut until he came upon a fence with a sign that read: "Military Reservation. Keep Out." When he turned the T-6 around, he hung the right wing and aileron on a fence post.

He saw the beacon on the base water tower so he headed for it. An officer in the control tower had not heard from him in some time and called him on the radio and asked him if he was all right. The cadet answered that he was okay and would be ready for take off in a few minutes. Later he called the tower saying the tire on his left main gear was flat. The tower officer told him to cut his engine and he would send maintenance out with a new tire. The tire was changed, but because it was on the left side and it was dark, they failed to notice the other damage. He called the tower again saying he was ready to taxi out for take off. He restarted his engine but called the tower again saying his tail wheel was flat. Again the tower officer told him they would dispatch maintenance out again to change the tail wheel. They still did not notice the wing damage. He again called the tower to say he was ready for take off, but the tower officer said

Instructors at Reese Air Force Base, Lubbock, Texas, 1949. Standing, left to right: Lowell Reed, William Holmes, Bruce Pope, Bill Lonsdale, Bob Paulin, Bill Annear, Lloyd Hoxie, Maurice Kersey, Marvin Hall, Donald Karschner, Art Latimer, and Salvatore Nucci. Kneeling, left to right: Salvador Danna (KIA-Korea), George Hammerschmidt, Donald Brown, Bill Clay, Tommy Mills, Oliver Buschov, Norman Fowler, and Gail Noble.

it was too late and to taxi back to the ramp. He taxied back the normal way, parked the plane, and returned to his quarters.

The squadron commander had the cadet get into his Jeep and they followed his tracks. When they got back the squadron commander said he taxied through patches of weeds as high as the wing. He also taxied by big holes in the ground and through the salvage yard over boards before he got to the fence. Needless to say the squadron commander was very upset.

He asked the cadet, "What the hell were you thinking about?"

The cadet replied, "I was just puttin' along."

This story was published in the *Flying Safety Magazine* under the title of "Gullible's Travels."

Fortunately he missed the dry lake bed I got into when I was a cadet. I was lucky. No one found out about it.

As punishment he had to wear an arm band with a dumbbell on it for the balance of his time as a cadet. Normally they gave it to the cadet who pulled the dumbest stunt and he only had to wear it for a week.

He finally went to the squadron commander after several weeks and told him, "Wash me out. Do anything, but let me take this dumbbell off." The commander agreed and the cadet graduated with his class. He undoubtedly will never forget his experience. Will he tell this story to his grandchildren? Maybe.

Leaving the Training Command

By 1950, the RIF was continuing. All reserve officers with less than an outstanding effectiveness rating had been cut, and our Wing commander told us there were more cuts to come. It appeared that all the reserve officers would be gone. I decided that if I was to leave the air force, I would do it at my convenience. I flew a B-25 to Andrews Air Force Base in Washington D.C., and went to the Pentagon to review my records. A colonel in charge of the records section reviewed my records with me and told me that they were all outstanding and I should forget the RIF because things were heating up in Korea and there would be no more RIFs, in fact, they were going to start recalling the reserves.

Shortly after I returned to Lubbock a reserve unit from the Los Ange-

Training B-25, mounted at the gate to Reese Air Force Base, Lubbock, Texas. The B-25 gained fame in the Billy Mitchell raid over Tokyo in 1942.

les area was recalled. They had all been given promotions to captain or major after the war as an incentive to join the reserves. Officer's and most NCO's promotions for those of us on active duty had been very limited or frozen since World War II. I was still a first lieutenant with more than six years in grade and had more than four thousand hours of flying time. Most of the reserves had not flown since the war, and by their own admission, their drill periods were spent "drinking and telling war stories." We flew with our students for half a day and re-taught the reserves how to fly the other half of the day. At one time I had sixteen students. After we checked them out, they became our bosses because they outranked us. There was a lot of frustration. This was a bit much to take, so I decided to leave the Training Command and see if I could find a better chance for advancement.

Except for the lack of promotions and the RIF, I enjoyed my tour. It was satisfying to turn out professional pilots. I could get one of the planes on weekends for personal use and I got a lot of flying time in the B-17 and the B-25. I enjoyed the B-17 because it is easy to fly, except in a crosswind with that big vertical stabilizer. Later the air force was broke again and we had to teach instruments in a T-6. I hated that little thing. I had not flown a single engine aircraft since basic flying school eight years earlier.

Our students had been training in the T-6 for the prior six months and had become proficient in them. I was given about three hours flying time to learn how to land one and then was given four students to teach to fly instruments in it. I had no problem teaching instruments, as they are basically the same in all aircraft. My problem was getting the aircraft on the ground and it did not take the students long to realize I was fighting for survival. I could not understand why my landings were so bad. After landing I turned off the runway and went through the after-landing check. Everything was normal. After graduation the students confessed that just prior to landing they retracted the wing flaps and we would drop like a rock. While I was trying to recover, they would ease the flaps back down. They got quite a laugh while I taxied back to the ramp shaking my head. Just before I left, the T-6 was being replaced by the T-28, which I got to fly a few times.

AOB Training

Our next door neighbor at Reese was the base personnel officer. He gave me a list of schools that were available. One school that interested me was for foreign air missions. The air force was sending a pilot, a navigator, a bombardier, and a radar operator to some of the missions in foreign countries. To save money, a decision was made to train a pilot in the other positions, so that one person could be sent instead of four.

I had received a promotion to captain in December of 1950, and met all the qualifications for the school except that I did not have a college degree. However, I did have three years of aeronautical engineering at Texas A&M and had taken courses at Centennary University while stationed at Barksdale Air Force Base near Shreveport, Louisiana, and at Texas Tech University while stationed at Reese Air Force Base near Lubbock, Texas. I had also taken some correspondence courses from the Air Force Institute of Technology. My neighbor said I should apply anyway, which I did.

A couple of evenings later at happy hour at the Officers' Club, I ran into one of my former Wing commanders who asked me what I was doing. I told him I was waiting to go to this school. He told me that there had been some changes made and that Gen. Curtis LeMay was taking the graduates for his SAC's new B-47s, which were just coming into the inventory. The name of the school had been changed to Aircraft Observer/Bombardier (AOB); however, the purpose of the school remained the same. This did not sound so bad. Although the project was highly classified, I had seen a B-47 once through a hanger window at Wright-Patterson Air Force Base at Dayton, Ohio. At the time I did not know what it was, but knew I sure would like to fly it. Later that night my neighbor told me he had walked my application through Training Command Headquarters and gotten it approved.

Our number three son, Jack, made his appearance on February 28, 1951, and was two weeks old when the orders came. We had a week to pack, clear the base, and get moved, this time to Houston. We moved in with Eva's parents for about three weeks until we found a house to buy. We finally had a three-bedroom house and with three boys, we needed it. At last, a home of our very own.

I reported for the navigation portion of the school at Ellington Air Force Base south of Houston, in March, 1951. Pilots were given mostly celestial and radar navigation training with a review of dead reckoning. The course lasted six months. After receiving my navigator's wings, I was sent to Mather Air Force Base, Sacramento, California, in November that year to continue bombing and radar training. The school was only going to last for six months, so I left Eva and the boys in our house in Houston. It was better than trying to find a place to live out there for six months.

The bombardier training was strictly out of World War II, dropping 100-pound sand-filled bombs out of a B-25, using the Norden bomb sight. It was fun, but the B-47 did not have a Norden bomb sight.

We had a spell of bad weather and it was necessary to make up the lost missions on Sundays. All students reported to student operations and waited to be assigned to an aircraft. When my aircraft became available, I went out to preflight it and wait for my instructor. While I was waiting, a B-25 came in on its final approach with its right engine feathered. When it was a short distance from touchdown, a B-29 pulled out onto the runway blocking its path. The B-25 pilot added full power to the left engine. This was a perfect example of what not to do under the circumstances. The unbalanced thrust of the left engine at low air speed caused the plane to start an uncontrolled turn to the right. As it passed over our student operations, the right wing hit the roof causing the aircraft to spin around and it landed on top of the stockade causing the roof to collapse.

The prisoners had just had lunch and were sitting on their bunks. When the fire trucks arrived, the driver hesitated because he was afraid to break through the fence because that would let all the prisoners out. Someone jumped up on the fire truck and ordered him to break through the fence. The flight crew managed to escape through the hatch between the two pilots on top of the plane.

One of my classmates ran over to help and was looking through a window in the stockade telling someone on the collapsed roof where to chop to reach the prisoners and help get them out. About that time the B-25 exploded. My classmate was blown up against a fence and a stretcher landed on top of him saving his life. When the aircraft exploded I saw one of the firemen, who was standing on top of the plane, thrown about ten feet into the air and come down into the fire. All of the prisoners were burned to death as well as those standing by trying to help. People took off running to escape the explosion. Later my instructor came out to where I was standing by my aircraft and told me he was stampeded by people trying to get out of the way. When he turned around, I could see a foot print right in the middle of his back.

The radar training was both navigation and bombing using a K-1 system that was used in the B-29. The entire school lasted a year. During that time I flew B-25s as a mission pilot flying students to get my required flying time for flight pay.

chapter 8

Strategic Air Command and the Cold War

I GRADUATED in April, 1952, from the AOB school and received my bombardier and radar wings. I received orders to the 49th Bomb Squadron, 2nd Bomb Wing stationed at Hunter Air Force Base, Savannah, Georgia. I went by Houston to pick up Eva and the boys. We took a little leave, rented our house, said good-bye to our parents, and headed for Savannah.

Traveling with a family in those days was a real challenge. We had traded our 1940 Pontiac that we bought in Denver for a 1948 Nash. They were one of the first cars to be manufactured after the war. There were no four-lane divided highways then, and very few motels. So with three little ones in tow, ages fifteen months to five years, we headed down old Federal Highway 90, which took us to Jacksonville and then took Highway 105 to Savannah. It took us three days. We arrived there on May 23, 1952, eight years to the day after I graduated from pilot training.

The 2nd Bomb Wing was an old unit and most of the top air force commanders in the bomber business, at one time or another, passed through the 2nd Bomb Wing. It was a nuclear unit equipped with B-50s. The B-50 was a larger version of the B-29 with larger engines. In addition, it had a jet engine under each wing used on takeoff and high-altitude cruising.

When I checked into the Wing, I was told not to unpack, that I would be moving in six weeks. I was not told where. Several of the people I graduated from AOB school with also received assignments to the 2nd Bomb Wing. We were there about three months during which time I got a couple of flights in a B-50. Again we received orders to move. This time, however, it was just across the base to the 375th Bomb Squadron of the 308th Bomb Wing. I, for one, had been looking forward to moving away from Savannah. There was no place to live. The 2nd Bomb Wing had just transferred in from Travis Field on the north side of Savannah. The 308th Bomb

Wing had just moved in from Smokey Hill Air Force Base in Kansas. Everyone was looking for a place to live. The city was not prepared for this influx of people. We finally bought a little house that had been repossessed and renovated by the Veterans Administration. It was small, but we were glad to get it. We lived there four years, longer than we had lived anywhere so far.

The 308th Bomb Wing was equipped with B-29s scheduled to carry conventional bombs. When I checked into the squadron, I was shocked to see the condition it was in. After seeing the smooth operations of the Training Command units and the 2nd Bomb Wing, I could not believe what I saw. All of the aircraft were grounded for one reason or another. Most of the flight crews, which had just been recalled to active duty, could not be found, and no one had seen the squadron commander who had been recalled to active duty from the reserves. How he held his command was hard to say because he was drunk most of the time. The operations officer had been on active duty since World War II with the exception of a short period of flying for Chinese Air Transport before returning to active duty. He was a very capable person. He told me we were the third wing in line for conversion from B-29s to B-47s. When that would take place no one knew exactly, but it would be at least a year. In the meantime we were stuck with what we had to try to develop a combat unit. We were to continue receiving pilots from the AOB and navigators were being sent to the bombardier and radar schools. The new B-47 was to have

B-50, 49th Bomb Squadron, 2nd Bomb Wing, 2nd Air Force, Hunter Air Force Base, Savannah, Georgia, 1952.

three crew members—an aircraft commander (formerly called a pilot), a pilot (formerly called a co-pilot), and a radar/navigator/bombardier called bomb/nav or observer.

The B-29s had been taken out of storage and were in poor condition. We were assigned regular air force maintenance people, and with a lot of effort on their part, we began to get the aircraft in shape. Getting the flight crews in shape was another matter. It was difficult to find a complete crew when an aircraft was ready for flight. Shortly after I arrived in the 308th Bomb Wing, I happened to walk by the operations officer's door. He called me into his office and said he could not find a regular bombardier for a B-29 that was getting ready to start its engines. He asked me to fly as a bombardier and drop ten 100-pound practice bombs. I told him I would be glad to, except I did not know anything about the B-29 bombing system and did not even know how to open the bomb bay doors. He said he would send an instructor to teach me the system.

My instructor was a lieutenant colonel. Even though there is an old air force saying that "there's nothing as worthless as the runway behind you, the altitude above you, and a field-grade (major through colonel) bombardier," I thought with his help, I would learn the B-29 bombing system.

After takeoff we climbed to an altitude of about 25,000 feet and headed for the bomb range. While en route I checked over the bombing system and found it was about the same as the bombardier school B-25s, computed the data to set into the Nordan bomb site, and handed them to the instructor. He said they were wrong and recomputed them and passed them back to me. I checked his and they were wrong. We finally agreed on the computations and dropped the bombs. After we made our bomb runs, I noticed my instructor was flying the plane. As it turned out he was a pilot who had graduated in the class ahead of me in bombardier school and this was his first flight in a B-29 also. The bombs I dropped had a good circular error (CE), meaning how far from the center of the target. So, for the next few months, I flew as a bombardier, which was a real problem for me considering the caliber of the recalled pilots.

Then came the real shocker. We received orders from SAC headquarters to take the Wing to Sidi Slimane, Morocco, near Port Layote in North Africa, for three months! We were to ground-stage through Kindley Air Base in Bermuda and Lages Air Base in the Azores. I was sent over early to set up the reception of the squadron. There were no major problems on the way over. During the three months, we did a lot of flying and worked long hours. There was no place to go on the edge of the desert.

On one flight I was flying as a bombardier dropping practice bombs at a target near Ksar es Souk, a French Foreign Legion post on the edge of the desert south of the Atlas Mountains. I thought I released one bomb and said, "Bombs away."

The radio operator who was monitoring the releases said, "It didn't fall." About five to ten seconds later, he said, "There it goes."

I never knew what caused the delay or never really wanted to know because the bomb hit in the middle of a herd of goats. The goats took off in every direction. Fortunately this ended my career as a bombardier. I will bet when our government paid for damages, those old goats on the edge of the desert were some of the "finest angora goats" in all of Morocco.

As we were starting to return to the States, the operations officer had all he could handle of the drunken squadron commander, and told him he quit, and took the first B-29 back to Hunter. The squadron commander then came to me and told me I was the new operation's officer and to get the squadron back home. Then he and one of the weaker crews all got drunk. He got so drunk, in fact, we had to tie him in bed with a blanket. The next day, between the maintenance officer and me, we were able to get all the aircraft in the bomber stream off as scheduled, except one. I held that one back to give the drunks a chance to sober up.

The following day it was necessary for the now sober crew to test-fly the aircraft before taking off for Lages Air Base in the Azores to join the rest of the squadron. After landing from the test flight, the aircraft commander reported that the throttle for the number three engine slipped back, giving an indication that the engine was losing power. The maintenance officer offered to have the throttle lock repaired, but the crew said the copilot would hold the throttle forward on takeoff. I agreed, because that is part of the copilot's duties on takeoff.

The navigator was so angry with the crew for their behavior that he refused to navigate and the ill-fated crew got lost on the first leg to Lages and had to be led in by Air Rescue. The next morning, taking off from Lages, the squadron commander was at the controls in the aircraft commander's seat and the aircraft commander was in the copilot's seat. Neither were qualified in those positions. They cartwheeled on take off. The accident investigation proved it was due to pilot error. Even though the aircraft commander was aware of the problem with the throttles, he neglected to hold them forward.

When they were taking off the squadron commander said, "We're losing number three!" He pulled the throttle back and hit the feathering button. The flight engineer said, "There is nothing wrong with number three." Then, he pulled the feathering button out. Even though the aircraft commander, flying as copilot, knew about the throttle slipping, he neglected to push the throttle forward. The bombardier, who survived the crash, said the two pilots froze on the controls and took no action to correct the situation. The squadron commander and the aircraft commander were killed along with five others. It was pilot error. There was nothing wrong with the aircraft. The accident investigation proved it was the fault of the two pilots.

In a way I felt some degree of responsibility. Had I gone to the Wing commander and told him the situation, it might have been prevented. I did, however, vow that I would never let an unqualified pilot or even one with minimum qualifications ever fly one of our aircraft and I would never let anyone touch an aircraft that had been drinking within eighteen to twenty-four hours of takeoff.

Shortly after we returned to Hunter, we were told we would start converting to B-47s. Our aircraft would start coming off the production line in about three months. In the meantime we would be sent to transition school to learn to fly them. While we were waiting to go to school, we were sent to survival school at Stead Air Force Base, Reno, Nevada. The school was run by the people who interrogated prisoners of war. They could be very rough and were to those who were caught on escape-and-evasion tests or attempting simulated border crossings. Rank meant nothing. Fortunately, I did not get caught. I managed to sneak across the border, meaning that I was safe from capture. As I was walking along, a truck load of the prisoners passed by and half our squadron was in it headed to the stockade for interrogation. They gave me a ride, but I did not have to go to the stockade.

One of my friends was captured. They made him strip off all his clothes and get in the back of a Jeep to be taken to interrogation. While en route, he jumped out of the back of the Jeep and disappeared into the brush. The guards chased him down and again put him in the back of the Jeep. All the poor guy got out of it was a bunch of scratches in embarrassing places.

One of our group claimed he got separated from the rest of us during the escape-and-evasion problems and that he was chased by a wolf. He came to a road and hitchhiked into Reno where he spent two nights in a motel and then took a taxi out to the base. You may believe the story about the wolf, but I do not. I knew the individual.

After returning to Hunter Air Force Base we found there was a delay receiving the B-47s. Since we would only carry nuclear weapons, we were sent to Bomb Delivery School at Sandia Base near Albuquerque, New Mexico. When we reported for class, I was talking to a group of guys in the back of the room. The instructor, who was ready to start the class said, "Will the guy, who used to paste beer labels on monkey's butts in San Antonio, shut up." When I heard that, I knew he was talking about me.

Back in San Antonio during preflight when we went into the city on one of our few open posts, we went to a restaurant on the River Walk, which had a patio with a wall around it. There was a jungle scene painted on the wall that had monkeys hanging from the trees. We took labels from the beer bottles and pasted them on the monkey's behinds. I looked up to see an old friend who was with me on one of those trips and who pasted a few labels himself.

This was a very sobering school. The weapon we trained on was the Mark-4 atomic bomb. It was three times more powerful than those dropped on Japan. That day I flew over Nagasaki while it was burning, I had no idea that in the future I would be carrying bombs far more destructive. We learned how to arm them in flight, how to prepare them to be dropped, and how to escape the impact. To do this, we were required to memorize the weapon's wiring diagrams in case of an emergency. The school lasted about six weeks.

When we got back to Hunter, we found many changes had taken place. The B-47 projection was back on schedule. We had been relieved of any combat responsibility, and we had been designated as a training wing. The gunners were all being trained in different fields because gunners, as we knew them, were almost a thing of the past. The B-47 had two 40-mm machine guns in the tail, but the pilot (formerly copilot) reversed his seat aft and fired the guns by radar. The B-47 had tandem seats for the aircraft commander and the pilot with the observer below them in the nose. We were scheduled to have an airborne refueling KC-97 tanker squadron added to the wing to support three B-47 squadrons. Most of the B-29 officers and flight engineers were transitioned into KC-97s or sent to school to cross-train for reassignment to B-47s.

After being home for a short time we were off again. This time it was to B-47 transition to learn to fly the aircraft at Pinecastle Air Force Base near Orlando, Florida.

I had been building a garage and workshop at home. The night before I left for transition, I worked late to make my project weather proof and kid proof. My next door neighbor came over to help me. He used the ladder and I stood on the kitchen stool. The leg on the stool collapsed and I fell, hit my head, and was unconscious for a few moments.

After I got to transition, I started having headaches, which I attributed to the fall, so I went to see the flight surgeon. I walked into his office and the young airman at the reception desk was leaning back in his chair reading a comic book. He looked up at me without saying a word and went back to reading his comic book. I said in a commanding voice, "Get off your ass and stand at attention when you are being addressed by an officer." I felt I deserved common courtesy, especially those due a captain in the U.S. Air Force. We had a very harsh discussion about customs in the military service in which I did all of the talking. When I went in to see the flight surgeon, who was also a captain, he tested my eyes and told me to come back in a week to pick up new glasses.

I went back the next week and went through the same routine with the clerk. I picked up the glasses and returned to duty. I had been flying every day. A couple of weeks later I found orders in my mailbox in the squadron orderly room grounding me. If I had had an aircraft accident during the period, the accident would not have been in line of duty, meaning that I could have been court-martialed.

I went directly to the flight surgeon's office. The clerk still had his feet on the desk, but I did not stop to talk to him. I went into the flight surgeon's office. I asked, "Why in hell did you ground me?"

He said, "Because you're irritable. You chewed out my clerk."

I said, "If I ever come back in here and get the same treatment, I won't say a word to your clerk, but I'll chew your ass out. Now, goddamit, put me back on flying status right now!"

With that, the flight surgeon jumped up to attention and said, "Yes, Sir." When I left the clerk was also at attention. I pointed to him and said, "You remember me. The next guy may be a bigger son-of-a-bitch than I am." and he answered, "Yes, Sir."

I guess they had never dealt with a very, very mad line officer before. I believe I hold the distinction of being the only U.S. Air Force pilot who was ever grounded for being irritable.

Most of the us had never flown a jet aircraft. Before we could train for the B-47, SAC had a requirement that we had to be jet-qualified. A bunch of young fighter pilots, who were rotating from Korea, were brought in to teach us how to fly a T-33 (a two-place version of the F-80). It was great sport for them to black out the bomber pilots. In my first flight,

Delivering the first B-47 to the 308th Bomb Wing.

my instructor landed the plane and I remember entering the traffic pattern on an overhead approach and taxiing off the runway—nothing in between. He made a 4G pitchout I did not expect and I blacked out. One time when I was flying solo, I decided to roll the plane for the first time since basic flying school over ten years before and the next thing I knew, I was headed almost straight down at more than 525 knots. I recovered and reaffirmed that I was not, nor would I ever be, a fighter pilot.

The B-47 training was uneventful once the differences between conventional and jet aircraft was mastered. One of the main differences was speed. The B-47 cruised about 200 knots faster than the B-29 and bomb runs were more than 10,000 feet higher. The speeds for each landing had to be computed; the B-47 was so clean that for each knot over the computed landing speed, it would float a little less than a thousand feet down the runway. Learning to land a bicycle gear (one gear truck behind the other) was a little difficult at first.

After completing transition, it was back to Hunter. This time we were able to stay home for a while. When we got back, the observers had completed their training and were waiting for us. Three-man crews were formed with an aircraft commander, a pilot, and an observer. The pilot on my crew had recently been recalled and was a very capable person who had been a pilot on a B-17 in England during World War II. The observer, however, was another story.

The great day finally arrived. I was sent to the Boeing factory at Wichita, Kansas, to take delivery of the first B-47 assigned to the 38th Air Division, which included both the 308th Bomb Wing and the 2nd Bomb Wing. As soon as we began receiving aircraft, we were ordered to make the Wing "combat ready" as soon as possible. To do this, it was necessary to continue transition training and to learn refueling from an airborne tanker. The observers needed a lot of practice making bomb runs on selected targets in cities throughout the United States. These bomb runs were scored by radar bomb sites (RBS) on the ground. To get this training started, SAC sent an instructor pilot (IP) to each squadron to assist in the training. My observer and I were one of the first to complete the training. We were designated as instructors and assisted in checking out the other crews.

As soon as all of the aircraft commanders were checked out in refueling, it was back to Sidi Slimane for three months. To make it to Sidi with

Turning the B-47 over to the 373rd Bomb Squadron. Left to right: Capt. Carl Weinmeister, Lt. Col. Vern Cammack, Capt. Bob Fisher, Capt. Al Stein, and the crew chief.

B-47, 308th Bomb Wing. Photo taken over the Atlantic Ocean off the coast of Morocco after giving an air refueling check ride, 1957.

a fuel reserve, it was necessary to refuel over Bermuda or the Azores. As usual there was a lot of flying with little time off. In addition to being an aircraft commander on a flight crew, I was assigned the job of chief of standardization. I was required to give all 375th Squadron pilots an annual instrument check, and my observer and I were required to give each crew an annual flight to ensure performance and regulation compliance. It was a lot of time in the air. Because of my memory of the B-29 crash in Lages, I failed a lot of people.

My observer was very capable; however, it soon became obvious that he had a bad drinking problem. One morning at Sidi Slimane, the pilot and I were getting dressed to go to work when the observer came in and started taking his clothes off to go to bed.

I said, "Wait a minute, you owe Uncle Sam eight hours and you're going to go to work." I told the pilot to keep him busy all day and not to let him go to sleep. He took Dexedrine to keep awake and would go out behind the building and throw up, but the pilot kept him working. I thought maybe he had learned his lesson, but that night, when we were getting ready to go to bed, he was all ready to go out and belt a few more. This is the sign of a full-blown alcoholic. After several attempts to get him straightened out, I finally gave up and had to have him discharged from the air force. Alcohol and flying do not mix. The last time any of us saw him, he was on the highway hitchhiking. He said he was going to Cuba to join Castro. I do not think Castro would want him.

Each quarter the Wing flew an Operation Readiness Inspection (ORI), which was a profile of our combat mission. Instead of flying over Russia, we made radar-scored bomb runs against targets in Europe and England, landing at Sidi Slimane in North Africa. These missions were also to test United States Air Forces Europe's (USAFE) fighter defenses. Each year we spent between four and five months at Sidi. We did this for about four years.

We were quartered in double Dallas huts, which were small plywood buildings shaped liked tents. They accommodated four to six people. The sides were screened at the top with hinged plywood that could be let down for bad weather. They had stoves for cold weather, but we never had occasion to use them, even though it got pretty chilly at night when the sun went down. The sand in the desert did not hold the heat. I do not remember it ever raining the whole time I was there. There was no transportation on the base except for the crews who were preparing to fly. The rest of the time, we had to walk. The food at the mess hall was served cafeteria style and was excellent. The cafeteria was air-conditioned and was spotless.

Anytime a group of men go off on missions away from home, some funny things are bound to happen. One of the funniest I remember was when a very good friend of mine, who shall remain nameless, was sent to Sidi Slimane on a mission. After he arrived, he ran into an old friend's wife. She was delighted to see him and knowing he was away from home, invited him to dinner. He graciously accepted and arrived at their house at the appointed 7 P.M. However, when the lady opened the door, she informed him that her husband was on duty and would not be home. My friend said that he understood and would come back at another time. She insisted, however, that he stay. Now my friend is a very good family man and very straight-laced. He felt uncomfortable with the arrangement; however, trying to be polite, he went along with it. She offered him a drink, which he accepted, and then she excused herself and went into the bedroom. When she came out, she was stark naked. My friend was so shocked, he bolted out the nearest door, which happened to be the back door, and ran smack into the clothes line. It took him a while to get over that experience. I am not too sure he ever did.

Sidi Slimane was about twenty miles east of Port Layote near the edge of the Moroccan desert. It was isolated and recreation was limited except for an occasional trip into Port Layote. As there was no other place to go during our time off, boredom was a big factor. One evening some of the younger officers decided to have a little fun at the expense of the Officers' Club manager. A couple of them faked an argument with the manager to distract him. While the manager's back was turned, another couple unhinged the doors of the men's rest room and took them out of the club. When the two who were keeping the club manager's attention saw the doors disappear out of the club, they abruptly walked away leaving the manager with his mouth open. It only took a few minutes for the manager to miss the doors. He ran out the door looking for the culprits and while he was gone, the two other officers took the doors off the women's rest room and disappeared with them. The club manager had the air police scouring the base looking for them. The culprits put them on top of the operations officer's desk as a joke. When the operations officer saw the air police combing the area, he put them on the roof of the 373rd Bomb Squadron Operations building.

I watched the whole thing. The next morning Colonel Tibbets came to my office and said, "I understand that the rest room doors disappeared from the Officers' Club last night and now I have to go explain it to the Base Commander. Do you know what happened to the damned doors?"

I said, "Yes, I know, but you really don't want me to tell you, do you?" He just laughed.

The doors were flown back to Hunter Air Force Base and mounted on the front door of the Officers' Club for the welcome home party.

When we first got our B-47s, our nuclear weapons were stored and loaded aboard the aircraft at Fort Campbell, Kentucky. You can see how ridiculous it was flying to Ft. Campbell, landing, waiting in line to have the weapons loaded, refueling, then taking off on our missions. Fortunately this only lasted until the weapons could be stored at Hunter. We took our weapons with us when we spent three months at Sidi Slimane. We did not take them when we flew over Europe because of the objections of the various European governments. Later they were stored at Sidi Slimane, making it unnecessary for us to bring them from the States. Needless to say, security was very tight and was continually being tested.

By now the weapon yield was four to five times those dropped on Japan and the weapons were retarded by parachute. There was no escape for the crew without those parachutes.

I was involved in one mission that could have caused problems at the top SAC level or higher. It was a simple quarterly rotation of the 308th Bomb Wing from Hunter Air Force Base to Sidi Slimane, Morocco. I was to lead one of the flights with four wingmen. The aircraft commanders were new and had never been to Sidi Slimane before. We were each carrying a Mark-6 atomic bomb. Our fuel load was about 20,000 pounds light to compensate for the weight of the weapons; however, we were to pick up the additional fuel from KC-97 tankers after takeoff. We were to meet the tankers at 15,000 feet, east of Charleston, South Carolina, on a heading to Bermuda. After takeoff I made a shallow right turn to pick up my wingmen. By the time we reached Charleston, we were in formation, but the tankers were not there. There was a front laying off shore, so to remain in the clear, the tankers headed north. I made radio contact with the tanker leader. He was over Cherry Point, North Carolina, headed north. By the time we caught up with the tankers, they were over Virginia.

After refueling, I headed for a point east of Bermuda to tie into our traffic clearance to head on to Sidi Slimane. To get through the bad weather, I put the flight in frontal penetration formation spreading the aircraft out further to avoid collision. When we were in clear weather again, we rejoined into a loose formation. We were scheduled to pick up more fuel from tankers out of Lages in the Azore Islands. I felt, even though we were a little short of fuel, the Lages refueling would give us plenty of fuel, and if there was a missed-refueling, we could land at Lages. At the time the weather at both Lages and Sidi Slimane was clear with unlimited visibility.

As we progressed, however, there was a slight deterioration of the weather at Lages. As we passed the "point of no return," where we would have had sufficient fuel to return to Bermuda, I contacted the weather station at Bermuda. They reported that the weather at Lages had deteriorated a little bit more, but predicted the weather to remain within takeoff and landing limits. We started running into head winds that put us further behind our scheduled flight plan. About an hour out of the Lages refueling area, I got a weather report from Lages stating the weather was "ceiling obscured, visibility zero, fog." By now it was night and we were really in a tough spot. Landing at Lages was out of the question. The nearest runway was on the Azores island of Santa Maria, but the runway was too short to land a B-47, and we did not have enough fuel to make it to Africa. All I could think of was the loss of five SAC bombers ditched in the Atlantic Ocean with five atomic bombs on board.

SAC headquarters that monitored the flights must have realized the position we were in and ordered the tankers at Lages launched in that weather. The tankers could hardly see to line up on the runway for take-off. Five of them took off to meet us, but their fuel to off-load to us had been reduced in weight because of the weather. Most of the fuel we were to receive would come from their own operating fuel. As we approached the refueling area, we ran into a driving rain storm. My wingmen pulled as close to me as possible. I had radio and beacon communication with the tankers. The main problem came in our descent from our cruising altitude of 43,000 feet to the tankers at 15,000 feet. Our air speed was 150 knots faster than the tankers.

I started the letdown far enough behind the tankers so that we were 1,000 feet below them. I could not see anything in front of us because of the rain, but we continued to close in on the tankers. We had to have that fuel. The lead boom operator said, "I think I see you." I started slowing down to refueling speed and we pulled in behind the tankers. It was a little turbulent and their "pilot director lights," which determine our position behind the tankers, were a blur on the windshield, but all five of us got our fuel in a short time. I began to relax a little until the tanker navigator gave us our position. We were almost to Santa Maria, not closer to Sidi Slimane. The tankers were going to land at Santa Maria. The runway was long enough for them, but the weather was beginning to go below landing minimums and they had given us their fuel, so they did not have enough to make it on to Sidi Slimane.

After we broke from the tankers, we took a direct heading for Sidi Slimane. We were more than an hour late and people on the ground began to wonder where we were and if we were still airborne. We ran into more head winds, which held us back even more. By the time we were about 100 miles from the African coast, we were at about 38,000 feet and I could see the light beacon from Sidi Slimane.

I made sure each aircraft commander saw it, and told them there was a taxi strip parallel to the runway that could be used to land on in an emergency. I told them to descend individually at 15-second intervals on my command. I was the last to descend. My "low fuel warning lights" were all on, indicating I was just about out of fuel. When I landed, two of my wingmen were still on the runway on their landing roll.

The people at Sidi Slimane knew we were just about out of fuel. They had fire trucks and bulldozers along side the runway with their engines running to push our planes off the runway in the event of a problem so the other planes could land.

After I parked, I just sat in my seat for a while unable to move. The mechanics used a rod to dip into the fuel tanks to see how much fuel remained. There was 3,000 pounds or 460 gallons. That sounds like a lot, but it probably would not have been enough to make a second approach to the runway. All of the following flights were canceled because of weather.

When the crews became combat ready, they were assigned a target in Russia. It was their responsibility to destroy it in case of an attack by Russia. My first target was Baku, a city on the west coast of the Caspian Sea where there were military installations, war materials, factories, and unfortunately a lot of people, too.

Intelligence, using spy information, U-2 fly-over photos, or any source of material, made copper plates from entry into Russian territory through to the target. Terrain features, such as mountains, rivers, cities, and towns, were formed by pressing them in from the under side of the copper. The plates were placed into a simulator that used sound waves in water instead of actual radar. The return on a radar bomb sight looked exactly like an actual bomb run. Observers were required to make runs on these plates until they were memorized. I was told that Gary Powers was shot down while flying a U-2 spy plane in our target area over Russia. He was to exit over Bodo, Norway, which is where our war plan called for us to enter Russian territory at the H-hour control line (HHCL). After dropping our bombs we were to exit Russian territory and land at selected bases throughout Asia Minor, called Jackpot bases. All of this was classified top secret at the time. I hope it has been declassified by now.

During one of our temporary duty (TDY) tours at Sidi Slimane, I was giving a flight check to one of the pilots. We were at a low altitude, at least 100 miles out into the Morocco desert, when we came upon a herd of camels. The two Arab camel drivers were having a fist fight. There could not have been another soul within fifty miles. Maybe that was the reason for the fight. Some people just cannot get along.

The Sidi Slimane Operations had a C-47 that was used primarily as a courier around the U.S. Air Force bases in Morocco. Occasionally it was also used to go to the British base at Gibraltar. One weekend a group of us decided to go to Gibraltar to do some sight-seeing. After we went through the old British fort in the famous rock, we decided to browse through the shops. We came upon a tailor shop that had very fine English woolen fabrics. One of our group bought a suit. I wanted to buy one, too, but I did not have my checkbook with me. The man at the shop said, "That's all right." He tore off a piece of brown wrapping paper and asked me the name of my bank. He wrote it out on the paper and said, "Here, sign this." I ordered a suit and a top coat. I had no idea if it would go through, but he did not seem to think there would be a problem, so I signed it. Sure enough, when I got my bank statement, it had gone through without a hitch.

In 1956, the 308th Bomb Wing had an inspection conducted by 2nd Air Force Headquarters, mainly of the Wing staff. They failed it because there was no one on the staff above squadron operations officer who could inflight refuel or who was combat ready. Very harsh and threatening words were passed to the Wing staff from Gen. Curtis LeMay. I was called to the director of operation's (DO) office and told I was being transferred to Wing Headquarters and would be in charge of the Wing Command Post and current operations. I did not want to leave my present job. He told me I would either come peacefully or under protest, so I had no choice. I think I was an instant fix for having someone involved in daily flying who was combat ready.

The command post is responsible for contact with crews in the air, where they are in their missions, and handling any problems they may have in flight. It is their direct contact with the Wing commanders and the Wing staff and where orders are passed on from the commanders to the crews in the air. They supervise the launching of aircraft and keep track of those aircraft during their missions. It is the nerve center of the Wing. It is also responsible for the needs of the crews on alert.

Shortly after I went to Wing, we received a new Wing commander, Col. Paul Tibbets, who had commanded the 509th Bomb Group and dropped the first atomic bomb on Hiroshima, Japan. Unfortunately, Colonel Tibbets gave me too much authority for a captain. It became known that I spoke for him. I insisted that some SAC and Wing regulations that had previously been ignored be complied with. This caused some bad feelings toward me in the squadrons. I heard one squadron commander say, "It's a hell of a note when a colonel has to go to a captain for a decision." I had to agree with him, but it was not of my choosing. I was complying with my orders. He later became my boss and I was in trouble.

Colonel Tibbets was the only commander I had in the air force who I felt would back me all the way if he thought I was doing my best with what I had available. I saw him back others the same way.

Late one night while we were at Sidi Slimane, I was driving a Jeep on the flight line when I met him walking. I stopped and picked him up. He suggested we go to the mess hall for early breakfast. While we ate, he told me about the atomic bomb mission and the preparation for it. I felt indeed privileged to be his friend and to work for this man. Later I read in *Air Force Spoken Here,* a book about Gen. Ira Eaker, the commander of the Eighth Air Force, written by James Parton, that when Tibbets was a major in the 8th Bomber Command, he flew copilot for Col. Frank Armstrong who led the first B-17 raid into Europe in a plane called the *Butcher Shop.* Colonel Armstrong later became a brigadier general and replaced the group commander of the 306th Bomb Group, an episode that became the basis for the movie *12 O'clock High.*

Just prior to our invasion of North Africa, General Eisenhower, his deputy, Maj. Gen. Mark Clark, and other staff members were in England trying to get to Gibraltar to take command of the invasion. Tibbetts was selected to fly the group in a B-17. It was raining and there was a very low ceiling. Many staff members thought they should abort the flight; however, General Eisenhower said he had to go because he had a war to run. Tibbetts flew at a very low altitude to avoid German radar and fighters. After takeoff General Eisenhower came up to the flight deck and sat on a two-by-four board suspended between the two pilots' seats. They drank coffee and made small talk and became acquainted. Tibbets became well known to the general staff and this led to his being selected for commander of the 509th Composite Group that dropped the atomic bomb.

One time when we were at Sidi Slimane, Colonel Tibbets came into my office and said he had to go to Paris and he wanted me to fly him. He told me to pick a navigator and another pilot because he would not return with us. The French would not allow an American nuclear bomber to land in France, so we flew out over the Atlantic and up to England.

As we were flying west of Portugal, Colonel Tibbets commented that the last time he flew in that area, he was in a hell of a fight with German fighters. He was on his way back from Gibraltar in a B-17, where he had flown Eisenhower and his staff to command our invasion of North Africa. The Germans found out he was returning to England and they tried to ambush him. I asked him what he did, and he said he just flew out to sea as fast as he could to get out of their range.

We landed in England where a C-47 met us to take us to Orly Airport in Paris. Before he left us, he made arrangements for us to fly back to England and did not care when we got back to Sidi Slimane. A chance like that only comes once in a lifetime, especially in SAC where there was such a demand on your time. We knocked around Paris five or six days until we were broke and then flew back to England. We got more money and decided to go to London. We spent four or five days in London, until we were broke again and then flew back to Sidi Slimane. When we got back, Colonel Tibbets was already back. I went to his office and threw my hat in the door. I told him I figured if he was mad at me for being gone so long, he would throw it back at me. He was not.

In his book, *The Tibbets Story*, he tells an interesting story about his acquaintance with Gen. George Patton. It seems that when Tibbets was just a young lieutenant at Fort Benning, Georgia, he went out to the skeet range one Sunday morning. There was a lieutenant colonel there also. They shot a round of skeet and the lieutenant colonel said, "I'll see you here next Sunday." The lieutenant colonel turned out to be George Patton.

There have been many interesting stories about General Patton. He was such a colorful character. Tibbets tells one though that I have not heard anywhere else. It seems that when Patton was a colonel, he commanded a battalion of tanks at Fort Benning. Patton wanted to watch the tank maneuvers from the air so he requested an aircraft from the army. They refused. Patton was very wealthy, so he bought his own airplane. Unfortunately he could not fly it, so he got Paul Tibbets to fly it for him. This was Tibbets's only relationship with Colonel Patton.

In his book he also told a funny story about Patton. It seems that his tanks were parading before a reviewing stand. Colonel Patton was in the stand with various dignitaries. He could not stand not being in the action, so he jumped over the railing of the reviewing stand, held his hand up, and stopped the next tank. He told the tank driver to get out and pointed to an old abandoned house at the top of a hill and announced to the crowd, "Watch this."

The tank driver said, "Colonel, don't do it."

He paid no attention. He started the tank and approached the house at top speed. The crowed watched as he slammed into the side of the house but he did not come out the other side. Pretty soon they saw him walking back down the hill. When he got to the reviewing stand, he said, "Nobody told me there was a basement in that house." He also said, "It pays to listen to your sergeant."

Promotions were still slow in the 308th Bomb Wing, but in July of 1957, I was given a regular air force commission with the rank of captain; however, I could not assume the rank of major until my thirty-fifth birthday on August 29, 1959. The promotion had little effect except I would not have to meet the majors' promotion board and I could stay on active duty for thirty years. All reserves were required to retire after twenty years. At that time I had been commissioned for thirteen years.

Our fourth son, Richard Karl, put in his appearance on December 10, 1957. We had been at Hunter five years and were active in a little Lutheran church in Savannah. We had bought a new house in 1958 and were very comfortable. The only drawback was the fact that I was gone so much of the time and had to leave Eva home to cope with raising our children. We joined a pool club at the Oglethorpe Hotel where the boys all learned to swim and we made some good memories while we were there, as well as lots of friends with whom we remain close to this day. The 308th Bomb Wing has reunions every two to three years and we have a great time re-living some of our experiences of our days at Hunter.

By this time both the United States and Russia had perfected guided missile systems. The problem was how the United States could be defended against a missile attack from Russia. This problem was presented to General LeMay and the SAC. Early warning systems were developed using radar sites all across the northern hemisphere. They could detect a missile being launched and figured it would reach its target in thirty minutes. In that thirty minutes the president would have to be notified and issue an order for the release of missiles from silos based in the United States, submarines on alert in the ocean, and SAC's strike force scattered throughout the United States.

The 38th Air Division, consisting of the 2nd and 308th Bomb Wings, was given the task of developing a ground alert system whereby seven B-47s and three KC-97s from each Wing would be launched, completely ready for our war mission, within twenty minutes of the time the president gave the strike order. The alert force was called Operation Reflex Action.

SAC bombers are very complex aircraft. On training missions it normally took an hour to an hour and a half to prepare for take off. Obviously some changes had to be made to comply with the 20-minute take off time that General LeMay required. Aircraft and crews were placed on alert status. When a new crew went on alert, they made a visual inspection of the aircraft, checking the chaff, ammunition, and the weapon. They ran a checklist up to "start engines." An auxiliary power unit, used to start the engines, was connected to the aircraft. After they completed the checklist, and the aircraft was considered ready for takeoff, a sign was placed in front of the aircraft that said "COCKED." An armed guard was stationed at each aircraft. No one was allowed aboard the aircraft except the flight crew.

Alert facilities were built on the flight line where the flight crews ate and slept. The aircraft were parked directly in front of them. The crews were given a combat mission folder that included maps to the target and any information about the target. When the alert signal was sounded, the ground crew started the auxiliary power unit. By the time the flight crews reached the aircraft, all they had to do was start the engines and taxi. Some of them even put their boots in the aircraft ahead of time.

The rest of the aircraft that were not on alert were to follow at set intervals. Considering the size and complexity of the B-47 and KC-97, this was no small problem. We were to be prepared to launch 24 hours a day, 365 days a year.

While we were developing the alert system, Klaxon horns, which made a very loud noise, were strategically located around the base. The communications people had a couple of horns left over and asked me what they should do with them. I told them to put one of them by base headquarters and one at Wing operations. They put one directly above the Wing commander's desk. When the first practice alert was sounded and the Klaxon horns went off, I was told the Wing commander was sitting at his desk and was not prepared for it. It was such a shock to him that he almost jumped over his desk. He came up breathing fire. The word got to me and I knew there would be another practice alert in a few minutes. The communications people asked me what to do. I told them to get that thing out of there immediately. They said there was not time and I told them to get a pair of dikes and cut the wires or whatever it took to get it out of there before it went off again. Sometimes you just have to lead people by the hand.

It took over four months to work the problems out. I am very proud of my part in developing the 375th Bomb Squadron and the 308th Bomb Wing into a nuclear threat. I am also proud of my part in the development of the ground alert system and the war plan. When the launch order was received, I was to go to the control tower, where I was responsible for the crews and ground movement of the alert aircraft. After the alert force was launched, I was to fly one of the follow-up missions.

One day after we had the alert force combat ready, a C-97 landed un-announced with General LeMay, several congressmen, other generals, and a task force of inspectors to test our readiness. An alert was sounded by SAC headquarters at Offutt Air Force Base, Omaha, Nebraska. We started launching the alert force, completely ready for combat, with nuclear weapons, ammunition, chaff to be used to jam enemy radar, and JATO (rocket bottles attached in a horse collar to the bottom of the aircraft that were fired to give additional thrust on takeoff and then jettisoned later). All of the aircraft rolled as required. Everything went perfectly. I was standing near a group of senators and congressmen who were discussing our operation. I expected to get some words of wisdom from some of the top members of our government. I did.

The head of the Senate Armed Services Committee said, "This is going to be like what the monkey said when he peed in the cash register. This is going to run into money." It did run into money because the ground alert system developed by the 308th and 2nd Bomb Wings was adopted SAC-wide and was in force for many years until President G. H. W. Bush ordered SAC to stand down in 1994, after the fall of the Berlin Wall.

After all the aircraft returned, General LeMay called all the officers to the base theater. We thought he was going to congratulate us and tell us how well we performed. From my position I could watch him with the congressmen during the launch, and I could tell he was mighty happy. When we were all assembled, he got up on the stage and said, "I'm taking five minutes away from you. You now have fifteen minutes to launch your first aircraft instead of twenty. And, if you are too dumb to figure out how to do it, I'll send some smart sons of bitches down here that can." He then turned around and walked off the stage. He was tough to work for, but he got results. He did not need to send the "smart sons of bitches" down there; we figured it out.

When I first arrived in the 2nd Bomb Wing at Hunter Air Force Base, the Wing had just failed an ORI. When the inspection was over, there was an officers' call at the base theater. Individuals who did poorly on the inspection were called up on the stage and fired in front of the entire group and given so many hours to clear the Wing and the base.

A normal mission without airborne refueling lasted about seven hours. With refueling, the length of the mission was based on the endurance of the crews. Once a year we were required to fly a mission called "Globe Trotter." These missions were a profile of an actual combat mission. They lasted sixteen hours. There were three air refuelings and it was necessary to attack a radar target in a city in the United States. On my last Globe Trotter, after about fourteen hours, my canopy split and I had to decompress the cockpit to keep the canopy from completely shattering. I did not have enough fuel to continue the mission at low altitude. I tried to get another air refueling but could not because no tanker was available, so I had to land after about fifteen hours and did not get credit for the mission. This meant I had to fly it over again. The missions were very hard because you could not get up and move around in a B-47. You were strapped in the seat the entire time.

While at Sidi Slimane I received an operations order from SAC headquarters to set up a B-47 mission to attack simulated targets in England and northern France to test their air defenses. I was not to file a clearance for the aircraft or reveal that these were our aircraft. When I planned the mission, I had the aircraft take off using light signals from the tower as there was radio silence. I had them fly at low altitude out over the Atlantic until they got out of radar range from Europe or Africa. Then they were to climb to bombing altitude, which was at 37,000 feet. The aircraft were to turn into the targets and mass-saturate the air defenses in Europe. When USAFE picked them up on their radar, they scrambled their fighter interceptors. I received a call from USAFE's fighter headquarters at Weisbaden, Germany, asking if they were our bombers. As directed, I told them I did not know anything about them. I soon got another call from a general, who said, "No shit, Captain, are those your airplanes? Because every fighter in Europe has been launched and are ready to shoot them down." Under the circumstances, I had to tell him they were our planes. Our test showed the capability of NATO's air defenses to be effective. I had been ordered to plan this mission and was pleased with its success although it caused some real panic for some people there for a while.

On another occasion I was asked to plan a mission for a flight of three B-47s to fly from Sidi Slimane to SAC headquarters at Offutt Air Force Base, which was not hard to do, but they wanted them to fly down the runway, in formation, at Offutt at a specific time right down to the minute. I planned the mission so they would be there a little ahead of time, but I put in a dog-leg so the aircraft commander leading the flight could estimate the exact arrival time. The SAC commanders were delighted when those three B-47s flew down the runway at the exact minute they had specified.

Our mission was to protect the United States against surprise nuclear attack by the Soviet Union. The Russians had warned that they would destroy us, therefore it was our mission to be so strong that they would know without a doubt that if they did attack this country or our allies, they would be completely destroyed. This era in our history has been called the Cold War. To fulfill our mission, it was necessary for the U.S. Air Force to be prepared. To accomplish this, the flight crews had to practice handling nuclear weapons. We never flew practice bombing missions with armed nuclear weapons on board for obvious reasons. If the American people knew how many SAC aircraft flying over the United States were carrying nuclear weapons, you would still hear screams echoing through the halls of Congress.

However, there were bound to be accidents sooner or later. I know personally of two. First, it is necessary to describe how the weapons were hung in the bomb bay. The Mark-4 through the Mark-15 nuclear bombs took up the entire bomb bay leaving only room in front of the weapon to arm it and room for a cat-walk on the left side for access to the weapon. There was a lug on top of the weapon that was attached to a hook (U-2 hook) in the top-center of the bomb bay. There were four sway braces, one in each corner of the bomb bay, that were tightened to the bomb to keep it from moving in flight. The U-2 hook could be locked electronically from the observer's position or in an emergency, it could be locked manually by inserting a tool that looked like a car jack handle, through a hole in the U-2 hook.

Operation Snow Flurry was an operation in which the entire 308th Bomb Wing was to participate. The aircraft were to take off at night in flights from Hunter Air Force Base, refuel from tankers out of Harmon Air Force Base in New Foundland, and proceed to Bruntenthorpe Royal Air Force Base in England. Each B-47 would carry a Mark-6 nuclear weapon.

I had been sent ahead to set up the recovery of the aircraft and crews and to assure security for the weapons. The Wing commander was in the first wave, so I met him and took him back to the command post to check on the progress of the second wave. One of the crews was listed as "missed refueling" less than an hour after takeoff. I knew that was impossible because the refueling area was about four hours after takeoff, so I called back to Hunter to find out what happened. I asked the Wing observer, who was on duty in the 308th Command Post, what was going on. He said, "I can't talk about it, but no one was hurt."

I began to suspect something went wrong with the bomb, so I called another friend in 2nd Air Force Command Post at Barksdale Air Force Base, Shreveport, Louisiana. I got the same answer from him. A tight lid had been put on whatever it was with a pat answer being given. He then asked me if I remembered a girl named Florence he ran around with. I did not remember anyone named Florence, but I did know that there was a town named Florence in South Carolina. The timing was right so I knew he was telling me that one of the crews had dropped his bomb on Florence, South Carolina.

Of course the bomb was not armed and there was no explosion. It hit between a house and a garage, both being knocked down by the wind pressure. A dog was near the impact. They say he took off running and the local people claimed he is still running. That one was pretty hard to cover up. The people in England found out we were taking the weapons into England. The "Ban-the-Bomb" groups were out in full force picketing the base.

When I ran into the pilot later, I asked him what happened. He said he took off with the weapon unlocked so that it could be jettisoned immediately, which was normal procedure, but he could not lock it electronically, so he leveled off and sent the observer into the bomb bay to put in the manual lock. The observer leaned against the bomb and steadied himself on the salvo cable and the bomb fell out from under him. I asked the pilot what he was thinking about as the bomb was falling. He said he hoped that dumb son-of-a-bitch went out with it. As a matter of fact he did, but at the last second he grabbed a bag that was lashed to the plane and pulled himself back in. That bag gave way too and he grabbed another bag. I understand he was in and out of the bomb bay three times.

At the investigation the observer claimed no one ever briefed him on the salvo cable. I was not at the investigation, but I personally told him how to manually lock the bomb, not to lean on the salvo cable, and what would happen if he did.

I ran into him in Vietnam years later. He had been flying with the "Ranch Hands," a C-123 outfit that was spraying defoliant at a low altitude. It was dangerous work. He asked if he could come to work for me. I gave him some excuse about clearances.

I was in Florence, South Carolina, in 1996. Everyone I talked to remembered the bomb. There was a display of it down at city hall. Sometimes it is hard to keep a secret.

The 308th Bomb Wing had the dubious distinction of having the man who dropped the first atomic bomb on a foreign country and the man who dropped the first one on the United States.

About the time of Operation Snow Flurry there was some talk about the British having to repay the United States for all of the equipment sent to them during World War II. After Operation Snow Flurry was over and all our aircraft had returned to Hunter, duty required that I go to another air base in England. I called for a staff car to take me to there. The weather was cold, rainy, and foggy. I had been working many long hours for the past three days. When the car arrived, I got into the back seat and went to sleep. When I awoke, it was daylight. It had snowed during the night and the sun shining on the new snow was a beautiful sight. I asked the driver, "Where did this beautiful day come from?" He said, "We borrowed from the Yanks, but, of course we have to pay it back."

The second time a bomb was dropped occurred also during a night operation similar to Operation Snow Flurry, but the 308th Bomb Wing was not involved. This time it was a B-47 Wing out of Homestead Air Force Base near Miami, Florida. As the B-47s passed over the southeast coast of the United States, they were intercepted by F-86 Fighters from the Georgia Air Guard on a practice mission. At the time I was on duty in the 308th Bomb Wing Command Post. The tower officer called me and told me that one of the F-86s had rammed a B-47. The F-86 pilot had ejected and the B-47 crew was trying to land at Hunter. The B-47 pilot wanted permission to salvo his weapon. There was no way I could give him permission. He knew his situation better than anyone and would have to make his own decision to salvo. I called his Wing commander at Homestead Air Force Base. When I explained the situation, he completely panicked and was no help, so I called the 2nd Air Force Command Post. Their controller would not give him permission either, but got the lieutenant general, commander of 2nd Air Force, and his staff on a conference call. Understandably, nobody wanted to be responsible for giving him permission to salvo his weapon. I was explaining the situation to them when the tower officer called and said, "Nevermind, he just dropped it." I passed the word on to the general and his staff. In unison, they all said "Oh, shit."

The general asked me to go get the crew; he wanted to talk to them. By then the B-47 was on the ground. The pilot did an outstanding job of getting it on the ground. It was in such bad shape, but it was salvaged. I took the crew back to the command post and contacted the general. The crew assured him they knew exactly where it landed so there would be no problem retrieving it. The navy dove for about six weeks in the silt at the mouth of the Savannah River and finally gave up.

In July of 2001, I was watching the news when it was announced that there was an atomic bomb in the mouth of the Savannah River. I guess the local people had found out about it and wanted the bomb out of there. The air force stated they could not find it and it had been there for more than forty-two years and there was not much chance of an explosion.

In 1957, the 308th Bomb Wing was on temporary duty in Morocco. The B-47s were at Sidi Slimane when the KC-97 tankers were at Benguerir, an air base near Marrekech, Morocco. I was giving a check ride to one of the pilots. The weather at Sidi was marginal, so we were shooting landings at Benguerir. The weather at Sidi continued to deteriorate, so I decided that we would spend the night at Benguerir with the tanker squadron.

That evening I went to the club and during some conversation with the tanker pilots, I heard them say they were way behind on their required quotas for transferring fuel. SAC regulations required a transfer 6,000 pounds or about 1,000 gallons of fuel to get credit for a refueling mission. I told the operation's officer to have a tanker over Benguerir at 15,000 feet, and I would show him how he could catch up on the requirements. I had learned how to manipulate the circuit breakers to make it possible to transfer fuel from the bomber to the tanker.

The next day I met the tanker as agreed and we were able to transfer fuel back and forth until they had reached their quota or we ran out of fuel, whichever came first.

When we returned to Hunter, 2nd Air Force sent an inspector to find out how it was possible to transfer more fuel than the tanker had on board. They obviously thought there was some cheating going on. The director of operations called me into his office and asked me to explain to the inspector how you could transfer fuel from the bomber to the tanker. When I explained to the inspector how I did it, he exclaimed, "By God, you can, can't you?"

In a few days we received a message from 2nd Air Force stating that in the future, fuel must be transferred from the tanker to the bomber. However, they did give the tankers credit for the refuelings.

In late 1958, the B-47s were being replaced with B-52s. The B-52 was larger, had better defense systems and more range, and carried six nuclear weapons instead of one. A top secret message came in giving advance notice that the 308th Bomb Wing was going to be deactivated and the crews were going to be phased into B-52 units elsewhere.

When I received the message, I called one of my very close friends and told him to come by my office. I had something important I wanted to talk to him about. I showed him the message, which was classified top secret, so the message could only be seen by a very few people. We had both bought houses in Savannah and we knew what would happen to the housing market as soon as the word got out that the Wing was being deactivated. We called a captain who had worked with me, but had been transferred to 2nd Air Force Personnel Center at Barksdale. We told him that we needed to go to the altitude chamber at Barksdale and asked him to send orders requesting that we go. We went to Barksdale and went by the personnel office to see him and explain that we wanted transfers and we wanted to know what was available. He disappeared for a few minutes and when he came back, he said, "There is an opening in the 72nd Bomb Wing at Ramey Air Force Base in Puerto Rico and an opening at Eglin Air Force Base in Florida for a flying safety officer." I took the assignment to Ramey and my friend took the one at Eglin.

He said, "Go back to Hunter and the orders will come through for you in a few days." We went back and swore our wives to secrecy because if the director of operations found out about it, he would have sent us to Africa. He did just that to one of the other pilots who was being transferred to California. His wife had to make the move alone. He was a vengeful character. We put our house on the market and started to pack.

I hated to leave our friends after more than seven years with the 308th, but not the Wing. Colonel Tibbets had left along with most of the Wing staff. Their mission had been accomplished and they had moved on. They were replaced by people who did not seem to care, and since the Wing was scheduled to be deactivated, some were just killing time until retirement.

chapter 9

Ramey Air Force Base, Puerto Rico

THIS WAS NO ORDINARY MOVE as from one city to another. This time we were going overseas, which meant we had to pack three different groups: household goods, which would go by ship and take two to three weeks to get there (hold baggage); items that we would take with us on the plane to tie us over until the hold baggage arrived; and the furniture and other items, which were going to be stored in Savannah.

Finally, on February 20, 1959, we left Savannah and drove to Charleston, left our car at the port to be shipped, and two days later boarded an air force transport plane for Ramey Air Force Base on the island of Puerto Rico. Eva and the children were very excited. It was the first time the boys had been on an airplane and of course the first time they traveled outside the continental United States.

When we landed, my new boss was waiting for us. He took us to temporary quarters that we would occupy until we could arrange for permanent housing. It was a long holiday weekend and the stores were closed, so he had stocked the refrigerator with enough of the basics to tie us over until Tuesday. He had drawn out sheets, dishes, and cooking utensils for us to use until our hold baggage arrived. Each base has a housing office that assists incoming families with necessary items until they get settled. It was very thoughtful of him and we really appreciated it.

It was the first and only time we lived on base. We were given our pick of several houses and were able to move in right away as it was completely furnished. It was the only time we did not have to get out and find a place to live. It was not fancy and was smaller than our house in Savannah, but we were so happy to be at such a beautiful base, we did not care.

Ramey was the garden spot of the air force. We knew a few people from past years and the new people coming in were SAC people who spoke the same language. We got a chance to go to St. Thomas and to Port au Prince, Haiti, for a weekend each. In Port au Prince we looked up a friend who was the U.S. air attache there. He showed us around the city and there was a charity ball at the hotel where we stayed on Saturday evening. We were in the company of the elite of Haiti. The president, "Papa Doc," was there and all the Haitian dignitaries. They were all dressed in their French-made clothes and finery. The food was also French and delicious. There is no middle class in Haiti. The people are either very wealthy or very poor as we found out when we saw some parts of the city. The government there is so poor that there is not even clean water to drink. It was sad to see such poverty.

Then we were able to take the whole family to Panama on an army transportation corps ship for ten days. Every weekend we took in some of the sights on Puerto Rico. When we went to Ramey, the boys ranged in age from fifteen months to twelve years. It was a great educational experience for them. They had the run of the base. There was a swimming pool, a stable where they learned to ride horses, little league baseball, and schools right on base. We lived outdoors most of the time. Eva had a maid six days a week whom she especially enjoyed because after Savannah, with me gone so much, she needed a little pampering.

President Eisenhower visited Ramey on his return from his tour to South America. He spent a few days there resting. That, of course, caused a lot of excitement. When he arrived, there was a parade on the base from the flight line to his quarters, which the wives had fixed up for him. When he got out of his car, our son, Jack, walked up to him. Ike shook hands with him and asked him how he liked living at Ramey. About that time a Secret Service agent escorted Jack away.

There was a commanders' conference at Ramey each year, which included all of the air force commanders. They had lots of good entertainment brought into the Officer's Club and we were able to take advantage of it. We especially enjoyed the local color, the Haitian Ballet, who performed the local dances, and the steel drum bands with their ethnic rhythms. At one of the conferences, the navy put on quite a show. They had most of the fleet from the area sail past in review. It was an impressive sight to see hundreds of ships going by.

The 72nd Bomb Wing was converting from B-36s to B-52s. The B-36 crew members were transferring out and the new B-52 crews were former B-47 crew members. The new B-52s had not been delivered yet and most of the crew members were at transition, learning to fly the B-52.

We did have a couple of C-47s for base support. I checked out in them and really enjoyed flying one again. There was not the pressure that went with the big jets.

Each week the honor squadron got the use of a C-47 for the weekend. Most of them did not have pilots, so about every four or five weeks, it would be my turn to fly them. I got to take in most of the islands in the Caribbean and Panama. St. Thomas in the Virgin Islands was the most popular with the young airmen who did not have enough money for hotels, so we flew over in the morning and back that night. The air force does a lot to keep the young airmen happy, especially those away from their families for the first time. There are facilities on the bases for recreation of all sorts.

In August, 1959, it was my turn to transition into the B-52 at Castle Air Force Base, California. I was gone about two months. While I was there, I put on my major's leaves. When I came back, it was the same as the 308th Bomb Wing—getting "combat ready," only this time we had people who came from B-47s, and it was just a matter of a different plane. As soon as we were combat ready, we set up an alert force with Gen. Curtis E. LeMay's fifteen-minute reaction time, only we started the takeoff roll at five-second intervals. Taking off that close together, you prayed the guy in front of you did not stop. In addition to my war-planning duties, I was given command of the alert force.

In alerting everyone on base when an alert sounded, it was necessary to put the Klaxon horns plus flashing red lights at strategic points around the base. I was given the task of telling the work crews where to place them. Because the chapel was on a hill and could be seen from almost anywhere on base, I told the people installing the Klaxon horns to put one on the side of the chapel. I got a call the day they were installing them from the base chaplain asking me to come down to the chapel; he wanted to talk to me. When I got there I saw a workman on a very flimsy ladder trying to put a Klaxon horn on the spire above the chapel. Of course I ordered him down. It gave the impression that we expected God Almighty to give way to alert vehicles en route to the flight line.

We finally got down to business. New B-52Hs began to arrive and the crews started returning from transition. I was assigned to Wing Operations War Plans. I had to attend war plan conferences at 8th Air Force Headquarters at Westover Air Force Base, Massachusetts, where I was given the targets in Russia that had been assigned to the 72nd Bomb Wing. It was my job to plan how to get them there.

The aircraft were to carry four Mark-28 weapons internally and two Hound Dogs (air-to-ground nuclear missiles), one under each wing. Each bomb had a yield of 1.8 megatons or 1,800,000 tons of TNT. Their destructive power was unbelievable. The nuclear weapons dropped on

Japan were 40,000 tons, and to think, in World War II, we flew for hours and carried one ton of bombs. The B-52 also carried four Quail missiles internally, which were decoys that gave the same radar reflection as a B-52 and were to be fired ahead of the aircraft while over enemy territory to attract enemy missiles. The B-52 carried a crew of six: two pilots, two observers on the lower deck, and facing aft on the top deck, an electronics warfare officer (EWO) who monitored and jammed enemy radar, and a tail gunner (usually a technical sergeant) who fired his guns by radar. The tail gunner position has since been eliminated.

It is needless to say that security was very tight. No one could get on the flight line without a line pass. In order to get one, a person had to be assigned to a SAC Wing. Security was a top priority to prevent sabotage.

One night I was airdrome officer and the tower called to say there was an unidentified aircraft on the final approach. After the aircraft landed, I went out to meet the pilot. It was a small single-engine civilian plane. At the same time, two flight-line security Jeeps pulled up alongside and stuck a 50-caliber machine gun into the cockpit. Needless to say, the pilot was somewhat shook-up. When I opened the door, he said, "I don't care what you do to me. You can put me in jail or anything you want. I was delivering this aircraft from Miami to San Juan. I have been through some horrible weather. I saw these runway lights and I thought, to hell with it. I'm going to land. Do what you want with me. I'm on the ground."

I calmed him down and told him to get in my staff car and we would take care of him. I took him by operations to close out his flight plan, got him a Coke, and took him to the BOQ. What he did not know was that during the night, the maintenance and security people took his aircraft apart to check it to make sure it was not a threat to security.

My parents came to visit us both Christmases when we were at Ramey and stayed for a couple of months. One night we had just dealt a round of bridge when we heard a B-52 take off. There was nothing unusual about that because they were taking off all the time. But this time the plane took off and suddenly became deadly quiet. The engines had stopped. I thought, "Oh my God," and then we heard an explosion. You could hear scooters taking off all over the base headed for the flight line. I did not go to the accident because I knew better than that, but I did go to the command post to find out who was on it. The deputy commander and the chief of the command post were among the eleven people on board. I lost some good friends that night.

It was a terrifying accident, especially for those on base. The plane barely missed the housing area and parts of the plane landed in a playground. Had it happened during the day, many would have been killed. As it was, no one on the base was injured. The investigation found that there was a runaway trim-tab that put the plane in a nose-high attitude causing the aircraft to stall. The pilot cut the engines and tried to bring it around, but it was too late.

The next day at noon, the base siren went off. This was not unusual because it went off everyday at noon testing the alert system. However this time, it did not stop, which was the signal that we were about to be attacked by enemy aircraft. I was home because I had taken some time off while the folks were there. I ran into the house, put on my uniform and my side-arms, and rushed out the door. I told Eva to get the kids and Mother and Pappy and get the hell away from Ramey because Ramey was sure to be a Russian nuclear target. It turned out to be a false alarm. There was a short in the siren. It sure did shake up the folks on base, especially after the night before. My mother commented, "I'm going home. This is too much excitement for me."

After about eighteen months we were given the task of setting up an airborne alert force, which consisted of one B-52 per SAC Wing. The planning was that the aircraft would be out of harm's way in the event of a Russian missile attack and would already be en route to targets at the command of the president. One sortie lasted twenty-four hours; there were two refuelings from tankers out of Bermuda or our own tankers and then one out of Lages in the Azore Islands. They flew almost to Israel before returning to Ramey twenty-four hours later without landing.

It was a very complicated mission to plan. Each aircraft carried three sets of information about targets in the Soviet Union. Each set had data for six individual targets to be attacked with nuclear weapons. It depended on where they were on the airborne alert route and the amount of fuel remaining as to which set of targets they would attack.

In the end, rotating SAC crews were in the air headed for Russia twenty-four hours a day, while SAC headquarters at Omaha, Nebraska, had an air force command post (Looking Glass) with a general officer on board in the air constantly, ready to take command in the event the ground SAC command post was destroyed. The communications systems and technology involved were astounding even in those days.

General LeMay's contribution to the Cold War is not realized by most of those who were not involved. The blockade of Berlin in 1948 and the relentless extension of Soviet power into Eastern Europe made Moscow's intentions only too obvious. On October 19, 1948, General LeMay was given the task of defending Europe and United States against possible surprise attacks by the Soviet Union by using the forces of air power in the SAC.

At that time, SAC had fewer than 52,000 personnel. It had 837 aircraft, including only 35 B-36 and 35 B-50 inter-continental-range bombers. It had only the beginning of a tanker force, with two air refueling squadrons just getting their converted KB-29s.

When General LeMay left SAC to become air force chief of staff in June, 1957, it had grown to a force of 224,000 active duty personnel, equipped with some 2,700 aircraft, including 127 B-36s, 243 B-52s, 1,501 B-47s and RB-47s, 742 KC-97s, and 24 KC-135s. It was the mightiest force the world had ever known. It was so obviously powerful that no nation could risk war with it. General LeMay saw to it that SAC was always ready to fight immediately—not the next month, not the next day, but within fifteen minutes when so ordered by the president.

I am very proud of the small contribution I made to this mighty force. I helped develop some of the procedures and wrote the operation's manual for the alert system. These manuals were used by the entire SAC ground alert force. Most of them were still being used nearly thirty-five years later when President Bush ordered both SAC's ground and airborne alert systems to stand down in 1990. The Cold War was over when the Soviet government collapsed. MISSION COMPLETED.

In September, 1961, just before school started, we had the opportunity to take a ten-day trip with the family aboard an army transport to Panama. We hired a guide who drove us around to see the sights including the canal and we did some shopping. We spent the night at the BOQ at Albrook Air Force Base. The next day we took the train back to Panama City for the return trip. It was quite an educational experience for Eva and the boys. I am sure they will always remember it.

After almost three years at Ramey, I received orders to Maxwell Air Force Base at Montgomery, Alabama. We hated to leave Ramey. It was so beautiful and we had so much fun with wonderful friends. We had a beautiful set of quarters and Eva had a maid six days a week. I had to literally drag her off the island. To make matters worse, some of our friends came to see us off with thermos jugs of gimlets. We did not want to leave.

chapter 10

Alternate Air Force Headquarters

WE FLEW BACK TO CHARLESTON AIR FORCE BASE on October 25, 1961. We had ordered a new station wagon and it was waiting for us when we arrived. Our old Plymouth was shipped back by boat and would not arrive for a couple of weeks. Finding a place to live in Montgomery was very different for us. There were plenty of choices. However, we decided to build a house the way we wanted it. It felt like home the first day we moved in.

When I reported to Maxwell, I was assigned to the Emergency Action Section of the alternate air force headquarters command post that was being set up in the event that the air force command post in the Pentagon was destroyed in a missile attack. It was established at Maxwell Air Force Base, the headquarters for Air University. The faculty and the students at Air War College and Air Command and Staff College had vast experience in nearly all facets of air force operations. In the event of a war, we were to be supplemented by members of the Pentagon's battle staff that were to be deployed to Maxwell. This plan would only be effective if the U.S. military forces were on an advanced defense condition (DEFCON) and had time to move the combat forces into preplanned positions.

We had all of the equipment that the air force command post in the Pentagon had, including the code to send the air force to war. We were armed at all times and had armed guards at the door of our only entrance. We monitored the bomb alarm system, which had censors to detect nuclear explosions at potential targets throughout the United States. Maxwell Air Force Base did not have these censors, but I could not help feeling that we would have been on the Soviets' target list because of our communication system. We had the electronic system, which was monitored by all arms and services in the air force, that would send the air force to war.

As of 1963 our function was to direct air force support only. During an emergency, the services—army, navy, air force, and marines—are turned over to the Joint Chiefs of Staff, and are to be directed from an underground command post in Fort Richie, Maryland.

Since I came from SAC I was placed in charge of monitoring SAC operations. Our group commander insisted that I obtain a copy of the Strategic Integrated Operations Plan (SIOP), which was the United States' complete nuclear war plan. I had worked with a portion of the plan and I knew SAC would never release the entire plan especially Annexes E and F, which were targeting and timing for the plan. Very few people had ever seen the complete plan for security reasons. I tried to explain this problem to the group commander, but he insisted. I wrote many letters, which he signed requesting a copy of the plan. I do not believe any of my letters were ever answered.

I worked on shifts and had lots of time off. It was nice to spend more time with the family. During the nine years in the SAC pressure cooker, sometimes I went for days and never saw my kids while we lived in the same house.

In 1963, I received my regular promotion to lieutenant colonel and was given command of the Emergency Action Operations. I stopped shift work, but still had a lot of time off. Squadron Officers' School, Air Command and Staff, and Air War College were located at the Air University. I gave briefings at War College and was able to complete the course in my spare time. It was the best school I have ever attended.

Each year the senior officer's schools from Maxwell, the Royal Air Force (RAF), and the German Air Force (GAF) held a seminar on new tactics and weapons. These seminars were hosted on a rotating basis. In 1964, it was the GAF's turn. I went with the Air War College group as far as Hamburg, Germany. There I left the group and was met by a German air force general who had set up an aircraft to fly me to Wiesbaden near Frankfurt. It was a cloudy day and I had seen the tops of clouds enough to last a lifetime. I thanked him, but told him I wanted to see Germany, so I took the Oriental Express train. What a fantastic train. If we had trains like that, our passenger trains would not be going out of business.

When I got to Wiesbaden, I briefed the USAFE battle staff on the continuity of the operations plan for the Department of the Air Force, which they had requested. The briefing lasted a couple of hours, so I was able to get in a couple of days sight-seeing before I was scheduled to meet the group in England. I got within ten miles of my ancestral home and did not know it. I ate in what had been a War World II German officers' mess. The walls were covered with pictures of ME-109s shooting down B-17s. My first roommate at Texas A&M, Ira (Doc) Pritchet, was shot down and killed in this area while piloting a B-17. How things had changed.

I flew on an air force courier from Rhine Mein Air Base to England. There I gave the same briefing to the 3rd Air Division battle staff. Then I met the Air War College group and we flew back to Maxwell.

As the alternate air force command post, the communications available were state of the art in 1963. Today, in 2003, they would be considered rather primitive. Our telephone lines were designed so that we could communicate with any military command worldwide. They did not go through commercial lines, but were dedicated circuits for use only by the military. We had the capability of monitoring or taping conversations if necessary. To prevent wearing a headset for long periods, we had a speaker to make it easier to monitor calls on our circuit and those going into the air force command post in the Pentagon.

This was at a time when all of the schools in the South were segregated according to race. Black children were not allowed to attend white schools. The black population was demonstrating in the streets for the schools to be integrated and for voting rights, which had been denied them.

One evening, when the University of Mississippi at Jackson was being forced to integrate by the federal government, I heard a Boston accent over the monitor requesting that we connect him to the head federal marshall at the University of Mississippi. The Justice Department had placed their federal marshalls at the university to control the integration of a black man named Meredith. When the head marshall got on the line, the Boston accent said, "This is Attorney General Kennedy. Tomorrow we are going to fly Meredith into the Mississippi National Guard Base at Jackson. At noon he will be brought in through the back gate of the university in a black car. I want you to create a diversion out in front." The head marshall said, "A diversion, sir?"

"Yes, a diversion," said Mr. Kennedy. "I don't want any interference when we bring him in."

That day there was a riot in front of the University of Mississippi and someone was killed. Of course, the students were blamed for it. I am sure Bobby Kennedy did not know I heard him order that riot. Had I said anything, it would have been denied and my military career would have been over really quickly.

I was in the command post for a period of four years and most of the days were routine. We were in the midst of the integration battle and witnessed the Selma to Montgomery March led by Dr. Martin Luther King. It was a brutal event for the people of Alabama, but its shock value proved successful for the black people of the South. The air force had been integrated for many years so we were not affected by the outcome. We enjoyed Montgomery and had a pretty normal family life for the first time in my air force career. But that was about to come to an abrupt end.

chapter 11

The Vietnamese War

AT THE ALTERNATE AIR FORCE COMMAND POST, we were on distribution for most of the services' war plans. It was quite a classified library. We had a captain running it. One day he brought an operations plan in for me to see since it could be in our area of responsibility to monitor. He could not believe it and wanted my opinion. I agreed with him.

Its name was Operation Phyllis Ann. The plan was for many of the twenty-five-year-old C-47s still belonging to the air force to be flown to West Palm Beach, Florida, where they were to be gutted and completely rebuilt. Then they were to be flown to Hanscomb Air Force Base, Massachusetts, near Concord, where classified electronic equipment was to be installed. Flight crews were to pick them up at Hanscomb and fly them on an easterly route to Vietnam. I felt the requirements when they got to Vietnam impossible considering the age of the C-47s and the distance from sources of supply. I could not believe the requirement of flying eighty percent of the assigned aircraft on seven-hour missions seven days a week. I laughed and said, "I pity the guy that is going to get that can of worms."

A couple of weeks later, a friend who was the director of personnel called and said he had an assignment for me. He did not know what it was because it was classified secret, but the code name was Operation Phyllis Ann. I told him I knew what it was and to get me out of it. He said, "The General picked you. Sorry."

I must truthfully say I did not want to go to Vietnam, especially because I knew the requirements for Operation Phyllis Ann. Also, I was not eager to fly an aircraft that was slower than the one I flew twenty-five years before in World War II, especially after flying jet bombers.

Eva could not believe it when I told her I was going to be flying combat in Vietnam and would be gone at least a year. By this time I was forty-two years old. She finally accepted it, however. No other choice. Air force wives are made of something special.

I went to England Air Force Base near Alexandria, Louisiana, for a briefing and a quick recheck in a C-47. I was given a special briefing on the eastern route from Hanscomb Air Force Base to Tan Son Nhut Air Base near Saigon, Vietnam. The route was to go to Greenland, Iceland, Ireland, Italy, Israel, Saudi Arabia, Pakistan, India, Thailand, and Saigon. When I asked why the eastern route had been picked, the answer was, "less over-water time and shorter distance between stops." I reminded the briefer that a twenty-five-year-old C-47 would depend on the host base for maintenance, many of which do not have C-47s and that it would be necessary to place air force maintenance personnel at each stop; secondly, the aircraft would have secret equipment on board and would have to depend on adequate security for the aircraft. Lastly, had there been any contact with the State Department about getting diplomatic clearances through countries that did not look favorably on our war in Vietnam? It did not look like a very workable plan to me and I told them they should think about putting long-range fuel tanks on the aircraft and going west and landing on bases controlled by the United States.

I was told I had to leave in July and was to arrive in Vietnam and get set up before the crews were scheduled to arrive. The route was changed to go through Alaska, so they would get there much faster. I flew on a commercial airline to Travis Air Force Base, California, where I transferred to another commercial airline under contract to the air force. So on July 2, 1966, I was back in the pressure cooker headed for another war.

Before I left, one of the master sergeants in my old office at Maxwell Air Force Base called ahead to one of the master sergeants who had been transferred to Clark Air Base on Luzon Island in the Philippines and gave him my flight number. He was a welcome sight when we landed. He took me to the BOQ to get a room. Then we took a tour of the base. I was eager to find our old World War II tent area. Everything had changed in the past twenty-one years, but I finally located the old Japanese runway where we had lived. It is now a park with big trees growing on it. In the area west of our tent area, where some Japanese trenches were located during World War II, the base hospital was now located. Things in Manila had not changed much since World War II except for the traffic. The streets were full of "Jeepies," many of which were Jeeps that had been abandoned and were decorated so they could not be identified.

Since I would be flying combat in Vietnam, I went through jungle survival training in the mountains west of Clark Air Base. To get to the training area, we were lowered from a helicopter hovering about two hundred feet above the jungle. I was in command, so I was the first one to go. I put on a harness and stepped out into space. Oh God, it was a long way down.

There were two groups of us. Another lieutenant colonel had charge of the other group. Each of us had a couple of officers and about a half dozen enlisted men with us. Before we left, we were asked what we wanted to take with us. The other lieutenant colonel said, "Everything we can carry." But I said, "Only what we would have in our pockets in case we had to bail out." My group was extremely worked up at me, but after we got down into the jungle, we survived on the supplies the other group got tired of carrying and threw away.

We were met by the Negritos, whom I had encountered in World War II. By now they could speak some English and wore fatigue shirts and pants, but still no shoes. They took us on a trek through the jungle and taught us how to survive by getting water from plants and showed us the plants that were safe to eat. The temperature was about 115 degrees and we perspired so hard that sweat would run in a stream from the bill of our caps.

We came to a beautiful jungle stream so I decided this is where we would camp for the night. The Negritos told us not to drink the water without using iodine tablets. The two captains who were with me and I took off our boots and jumped in the water in our flying suits to cool off. What a miserable night that was. The flying suits were clammy and never dried out. I could not sleep because I could see something glowing in the dark. I am convinced that it moved. It turned out to be phosphorescent plants of some sort. The next morning the Negritos took us farther up the river to their camp. This is where we found out why we could not drink the water—it was their sewage system.

I spent five days in the jungle and I developed a great respect for the men who had to fight a war in that environment. I have never been a great advocate of practicing being miserable. I did learn one important thing: *Keep the aircraft engines running and do not go down in the jungle.*

After I returned to Clark, I contacted a friend who was assigned to the Philippines Military Assistance Group (PMAG). He invited me to spend a couple of days with him and his wife in Manila. He sent a staff car to pick me up. On the way to Manila, I found it interesting to drive down the same road that I had traveled on during World War II, only this time, there were no snipers. We stopped at a small restaurant where I had been during the war. I had an interesting conversation with the woman who owned the restaurant. She told me that the Japanese had lined up many of the local residents and were prepared to shoot them when an American tank pulled into the area. The Japanese all ran and the residents were rescued. It was surprising that there were not very many changes in the last twenty-one years. I recognized many of the landmarks along the way.

After a few days in Manila, my friend made arrangements for a staff car to take me back to Clark. I caught a flight to Tan Son Nhut Air Base (TSN) near Saigon. When I landed, it was pouring rain. I was met by two lieutenant colonels who helped me with my bags and briefed me on the 460th Reconnaissance Wing. When I asked them about Operation Phyllis Ann, they said, "Aren't you coming to the 460th Wing?" They were disappointed because they had wasted all their efforts on the wrong guy. I guess they thought I was one of their replacements. They took me to the Phyllis Ann building and dropped me.

When I walked into the building, I found M.Sgt. Lester Layman whom I had known for many years in the 308th Bomb Wing. I asked him, "What the hell are you doing here?"

He said, "I'm the first sergeant. What are you doing here?"

I said, "I don't know."

We were fortunate to have Sergeant Layman as our first sergeant. He was one of the best administrative assistants in the air force. Back in the 308th Bomb Wing, he was the personnel master sergeant major. The administration of the Air Refueling Squadron was in very unsatisfactory condition. The Wing commander relieved the old squadron staff and transferred Sergeant Layman from Wing headquarters and an entire new staff to the Refueling Squadron to reorganize it. In a very short time the results were obvious. Sergeant Layman retired as a chief master sergeant.

I have kept in touch with him and count him as one of my good friends. When you had been in the air force this long, you had made a lot of friends scattered all over the world. I never went on an air force base where I did not have friends. The air force is a big organization, but a small community.

When I left the States for Vietnam, I expected primitive living conditions similar to World War II. What a pleasant surprise I had. The army was responsible for assigning quarters to all of the services. They assigned us to a new Vietnamese two-story hotel. I had one room with a private bath. The water was heated by the sun's reflection on the roof. However, by the time I got home in the evening, all of the hot water was gone, so it was either take a cold shower or go without. My room was furnished with a desk and a chair, a wall locker, and a bed with a night table. Each room had a ceiling fan. Sounds great, but the bed was a slab door on legs with a mattress of three inches of foam rubber. Fortunately I only spent about five hours a night in bed. The toilet seats were made of thin plastic for the small Vietnamese, and when big Americans sat on them, they cracked, so for the next year I had to be very careful that I did not get pinched when I got up.

Across the street was a little Catholic church. Every morning at five o'clock, the priest would ring the bell calling his flock to mass and then lead them in song. Of course it woke everyone up, but after a while, if for some reason he did not ring the bell, we woke up anyway.

I had a maid that kept my room spotless. Each morning my boots were highly polished and my fatigues were starched and pressed. My maid was a very good woman. She indicated to me immediately that she was a Christian. I found this to be true one evening when I returned. She hit me and scolded me. I could not understand what she was saying, but when she went to my bed and lifted my pillow, I saw that I had left my wallet in the room that morning. She was letting me know that it was not the right thing for me to do. She was a country girl who came to Saigon for security reasons. She was raising two children of her own and three of her sister's. Her husband was away in the Vietnamese army. One morning she found a box on her front porch, and when she opened it, her husband's head was inside. This was a very strange and cruel war. You never knew if the person standing beside you was an enemy. The person who decapitated him knew where she lived. I have thought of her often and wondered how she is getting along.

When I met with the Wing commander, he confessed that because of the classification, he did not know why we were there or anything about our mission. He told me if I had any problems to let him know. I did not see him again for several months. We were strictly on our own.

Operation Phyllis Ann began with the 360th Tactical Electronic Warfare Squadron (TEWS), which was attached to the 460th Reconnaissance Wing, 7th Air Force. Lt. Col. Jim Jelley was the squadron commander and I was the operations officer. He had a lot of experience with maintenance and my experience was with operations. It worked out great. He was one of the hardest working and finest men whom I had the good fortune to be associated with in the air force and we are still close friends today.

We were to build the 360th TEWS to full strength, and then divide the squadron in half forming a new squadron, the 361st TEWS, sending it to Nah Tran. We were then to rebuild the squadron to full strength; then again, split it to form a new squadron, the 362nd TEWS in Pleiku.

My job was to develop the operations. When I went to the building that had been assigned to us, I found it to consist of one room with wall lockers along one wall, a few chairs, and a table. There was not much to work with. The room was crowded with junior officers and airmen, and you could hardly see across the room for the cigarette smoke. No one acknowledged that I had entered the room.

I jumped up on the table and announced that I was the new operations officer and I ordered all the enlisted men out of the room. I had always been taught that in a situation like this, the first thing to do is establish a staff and get them working while you supervise. I began to interview the officers and assign jobs. I explained that there was a stream of aircraft coming from the States to Tan Son Nhut and it would be our job to prepare to receive them.

Communication is vital to any military operation. Troops on the ground must be able to communicate with other units. Radio transmissions are essential especially in the jungle. Our mission at Phyllis Ann was to locate Viet Cong (VC) units in the jungle by triangulating their radio transmissions and reporting their positions to Intelligence. This system was known as Airborne Radio Detection Finding (ARDF).

When the crews started to arrive, I am happy to say they were professionals. The younger pilots in the air force had graduated from flying school in jet aircraft. Not too many of them had any experience in a prop-driven aircraft. As a result our pilots were older, in fact, we were called the "Antique Airlines," and our squadron insignia was an old tiger sitting in a rocking chair. Some of our pilots were grandfathers. A crew consisted of two pilots, a navigator, a flight engineer, and three back-end or support crew members. The pilots, navigators, and flight engineers were assigned to the 360th and were my responsibility. The back-end or support crew members consisted of three electronic technicians provided by the 6994th Security Squadron to operate the electronic equipment we had on board. Many of the pilots and navigators came from the SAC. They were former B-47 crew members who became available with the phase out of the B-47s. It was not uncommon for the two pilots to have 15,000 to 17,000 hours of flying time between them. The flight engineers had been flying C-47s most of their air force careers. Since most of my experience was in SAC, I organized the unit like a SAC operation. I tried to fly once or twice a week giving check rides or as one of the pilots.

At first I had problems with the support crews, or the back-end crews. I insisted they were part of the flight crews, were to comply with my briefing and flying directives, and were to be under the control of the aircraft commanders. The operations officer of the 6994th Security Squadron did not think it was necessary. The 6994th commander was from SAC and fortunately agreed with me. The flight crews from the 360th Squadron and three intelligence personnel from the 6994th Squadron became integrated crews.

Our electronic technicians scanned the VC radio frequencies and when they located a strong radio signal, they would lock on to it. Then they would tell the pilot: "Lock on." On the pilot's instrument panel there was a gauge called Pilot Direction Indicator (PDI). The pilot would turn the aircraft so that the PDI pointed 90 degrees from the heading of the aircraft. The navigator charted a line of position (LOP) from the aircraft to the radio station. While the pilot maintained a heading, the PDI would move 10 degrees. Then the navigator would take another LOP. The pilot would then turn the aircraft until the PDI was again 90 degrees from the heading. This procedure would be repeated until the navigator had three LOPs. Throughout South Vietnam, there were geographic landmarks, such as bridges, road intersections, etc., the exact locations of which were known. The navigator, using his drift meter, guided the pilot over the landmarks and set his navigation equipment to the exact coordinates of the landmarks. By using this equipment we knew our position at all times and could locate the exact site of enemy radio stations. This information was passed on to Intelligence. In essence we were doing the same thing Uncle Robert was doing in World War I, locating the enemy and reporting their position back to Intelligence. Of course our equipment was much more sophisticated, but the concept is the same. Sometimes at night we would pick up a strong signal from a radio station, but were not able to triangulate it. Because of atmospheric conditions it may have been many miles away in China. We located one radio station northeast of Saigon that was constantly spewing VC propaganda. It was in a house and we knew the station was there, and flew over it many times. We did not attack it because we did not feel it was worth going after. There was another radio station northwest of Saigon that we could never triangulate. We believe that the transmitter was on a bicycle going down a jungle trail. The VC outsmarted us despite all our fancy equipment.

One day I was flying north along the Central Highlands when we located a radio station on a South Vietnamese army base at Ban Me Thuot. The VC had established a radio station there. Of course, the Vietnamese army did not know it was there. When we reported it, I guess they cleaned it out because it disappeared.

Wing headquarters, Tan Son Nhut Air Base, Saigon, Vietnam, October, 1966.

On another flight we picked up a radio station on a plateau north of Saigon. I called Paris Control, who controlled all military aircraft in II Corps or the area around Saigon, to send in fighters to knock it out. I pulled off to one side and the fighters came in and bombed it. During the bombing the station went off the air, but it came back on as soon as the fighters left. Then I knew they were underground. All I could do was pass it on to Intelligence.

Our equipment worked so well that when we passed our findings along to the army, they used it for gun laying. I also had a detachment, Operation Drill Press, that was stationed at Tan Son Nhut, but staged out of Da Nang, which is in the northeast corner of South Vietnam, and supported the marines near the demilitarized zone (DMZ). This unit was in place when I arrived, but I was given operational control. I was working directly for 7th Air Force Operations. That is where all my mission or frag orders came from. Operation Drill Press did not have our ability to triangulate radio stations. They carried someone who could speak Vietnamese and would monitor the stations and pass the information they heard on to the marines.

Our maintenance people were the cream of the air force. All the fears I had back at Maxwell about the aircraft requirements and maintenance were for nothing. During the year I was there, we never lost a sortie due to maintenance, even when the planes came back with battle damage. This, of course, was due to the expertise of our maintenance people.

I did have one bit of trouble. When the enlisted men came to the early morning briefing, I asked each one of them if they had breakfast. They answered, "No, the mess hall was closed." I did not worry about the officers because their mess was open twenty-four hours a day and they had good food. I could not understand why the enlisted men's mess hall was not open. I sent the doctor who was attached to us to tell the food service people to be sure the mess hall was open because I did not want my people going into combat hungry. He told them "that Colonel down there is breathing fire. You'd better get this mess hall open in the morning." A couple of mornings later I asked the crews coming in for briefing if they had breakfast at the mess, and they all answered, "No, the food is too greasy." Sometimes you just cannot win.

The author in Vietnam, 1966–67.

360th recon plane over the jungle in Vietnam.

I thought that perhaps we could get combat rations, but found out, because we were considered a static unit with access to a mess hall, we were not authorized combat rations. When I sent a Drill Press plane to Da Nang, I would put a bottle of whiskey on board. The young marines, who were not authorized liquor rations, would steal a truck-load of combat rations and deliver them to our plane for the return trip to Tan Son Nhut in exchange for the liquor.

I turned the combat rations over to our personnel equipment section and they would charge fifteen cents a box for the rations. The money would go to pay for the whiskey and for a party for the squadron. I gave one of the majors a pretty rough time for disobeying my orders. To get even he said, "I'm going to report to the Inspector General that you are selling combat rations." I knew it was illegal, but I was trying to take care of our enlisted men. So that ended it and I had to give away the rest of the rations.

There was an article in *Life* magazine about the 460th Reconnaissance Wing in South Vietnam. The article praised the Wing commander because he was in command of all reconnaissance in South Vietnam and in Thailand. The article called him "Mister Reconnaissance." He was really proud of that and his ego was greatly inflated because of it. The span of control of all the reconnaissance units was almost impossible. I believe that he really wanted to get rid of us to not have to deal with our unit. He gave us the excuse of his not having a security clearance for Phyllis Ann.

One day he had one of each type of plane assigned to the 460th Reconnaissance Wing lined up in front of Wing headquarters. He had the commanding officers and operations officers of each of the squadrons under his command at Tan Son Nhut standing in front of each aircraft. He was out in front posing with his deputy commander. Pictures were taken from every angle. He had made arrangements for a helicopter to come over and take aerial photographs of the group. The helicopter took one picture and he motioned for the helicopter to come down lower. Unfortunately it was during the dry season and a cloud of dust blew his dreams away. When he rotated back to the States, a going away party that all officers were required to attend was thrown by his staff. It was a command performance. We were all subjected to speeches praising him. The officers slipped out one at a time until there was only a handful left. What an egotist!

One day one of his small twin-engine utility planes landed gear-up on the runway. I was appointed as president of the collateral board to determine the cause of the accident. Our investigation showed that there was nothing wrong with the landing gear and it was purely pilot error. The pilot had simply failed to lower the landing gear. In my report I stated that there was a lack of air discipline because the pilot failed to use his checklist as required by regulation. The Wing commander called me in and told me to reconvene my board. He argued that I had not shown any final conclusions in my report. I told him he did not read far enough. Then he read the part about air discipline. He got very upset because this was a reflection on him. I was not one of his favorite people from then on.

When I was selecting people to man the other squadrons, one of the new pilots, Maj. Harry Patterson, asked me if there was any possibility of his staying at Tan Son Nhut. When I asked him why, he said that his son, Tim, was an infantry enlisted man with the 173rd Airborne Brigade stationed nearby, and he would be able to see him periodically. I told him that was good enough reason for him to stay. Later he came to me and said his son was coming out of the jungle and had a few days off and he wanted to know if he could bring him down to our billet. I told him to tell the boy to take off his uniform and put on civilian clothes and we would find him a place to stay with us. He was a real nice kid and we all liked him. After his leave was up, he returned to his unit.

About a month later we were having breakfast, and I asked Harry how his son was getting along. He said he was coming out of the jungle that day and he wanted to know if he could bring him back down to stay with us again. Of course, I told him yes. He went with me down to the squadron and when we got there, the mortuary officer was waiting. His son had been killed in a helicopter by small arms fire from the ground. This was a real shock to Harry and all of us. He was such a nice kid. We made arrangements for Harry to escort his son's body home. He never returned to Vietnam.

When I first went to Vietnam in 1966, the bodies of those killed in action (KIA) were given high priority to be returned to the States, but as the war progressed, the high priority went to fighting the war. One time when I landed at Pleiku, I noticed about a dozen bodies lying along the taxi-way covered with ponchos. When I went into operations, I asked about them. They told me that they had been there three or four days waiting for transportation to the mortuary at Tan Son Nhut.

The mortuary, which was attached to the base hospital at Tan Son Nhut, serviced KIAs from all of the services from all the nations involved in the Vietnam War. It was located in the center of the base and was not the greatest of morale builders. Fifty-five gallon drums of embalming fluid were stacked up outside the building as well as the shipping containers used to send the bodies back to the States, where they were furnished with caskets before sending them to their various homes. Outside of the area there was an incinerator where large stacks of blood-stained uniforms were waiting to be burned. Blood from the mortuary was drained into a ditch, which during the rainy season was flushed out. Otherwise it washed out periodically when the odor in that tropical climate became overpowering.

One day I was eating lunch at the Officers' Club, which was very crowded. A middle-aged civilian sat at our table and introduced himself as a senior mortician. He said this was his third war and went on to tell me that his "customers" were more mangled in Vietnam than they had been in the other wars. He told me a lot of other things about his trade that I really did not want to know. It is a dirty job, but somebody has to do it, and I am glad that somebody was not me. I am also glad I was not one of his "customers."

One morning when I was in the Officers' Mess Hall having an early breakfast in preparation for an early morning flight, a bus-load of new army warrant officers pulled up to the mess hall. One of the young warrant officers came over to my table and said he would like to ask me some questions. I told him to sit down and his first question was, "Where am I?"

I told him he was at Tan Son Nhut Air Base outside of Saigon. He said he had recently graduated from helicopter training at Fort Rucker, Alabama, and was shipped out immediately. They did not tell him where he was going, but he had a pretty good idea it was Vietnam. That is the army! He then asked me about combat flying. I told him as much as I could, but I did not have the heart to tell him the reason he and his buddies were there was because of the high casualty rate among helicopter pilots.

I was in my office when I heard a commotion outside and the sound of people running. When I got outside, I found that a China Air Transport C-46 had ground looped coming off the taxi-way. Its wing hit the nose of one of our aircraft knocking the nose about 20 degrees out of alignment. By the time I got to the accident, the base aircraft maintenance officers were inspecting the damage. One of them commented, "I guess we can write off one sixty thousand dollar 'goon' (slang for the C-47)." It would be necessary to get help from the States to fix it. When I told him that there was more than three million dollars worth of classified equipment on board, and they would have to post a guard to protect it, in unison, they all said, "Oh shit. That means we have to fix it." They repaired the aircraft, but it was out of action for a couple of months.

There were two sergeants working for me who were real scroungers. A scrounger in military terms is one who appropriates government assets or property without authority or permission. In civilian life, they would be considered thieves. An accomplished scrounger can be a very valuable asset if they do their scrounging for their unit and not for themselves. These two were both staff sergeants who had the very appropriate names of Hooks and Wires.

At Tan Son Nhut our operations building was between the runway and the ramp. There was no water in our area, so I told Sergeants Hooks and Wires to go to the motor pool, draw a Jeep trailer with a tank, flush it out, and take it to the medics to make sure it was clean; then go to the water point and fill it up. They had been gone a while when First Sergeant Layman came into my office looking for Hooks and Wires. I told him where I had sent them. He said that he had tried to get a tank trailer, but none were available. In a couple of hours the pair came back with a brand new tank trailer. I was delighted until a little while later when a very upset major came into my office and accused me of stealing his trailer. I told him we just got a brand new one from the motor pool. While I was talking, I leaned my hand on the tank and when I took it down, it had still wet air force blue paint on it. All I could do was tell the major it was his and to take it. We both understood the situation and laughed. Later when I got my hands on the culprits, I told them, "Forget the 104th Article of War (used for company punishment), did you two steal that trailer?" After a long pause, one of them said, "Well, let's just say we were present when it was appropriated."

Another time I sent the pair out for a conex box, which was a large metal container used to ship mail in and often left in Vietnam. I saw them coming across the ramp with a box on a fork lift and there was a very mad chief master sergeant right behind them. Fortunately he caught up with them before they got to our area, so I did not have to deal with the chief master sergeant. They not only stole his conex box and its contents, but they also "borrowed" his fork lift.

While we were setting up the 362nd TEWS at Pleiku in the highlands, the new squadron commander called me and asked if I could send him some help for a couple of weeks to construct some of their physical operation. I figured Hooks and Wires were just the pair he needed, so I sent them. After a few days I got a call telling me that they had stolen so much from the army that if they caught them, they were going to kill them and for me to get them out of there. I had a plane going into the area and had the crew pick up the pair on the road home. As it turned out the only thing they built was a "cat house" for the local girls right next to operations. I pulled them out before they had an opportunity to cash in on that venture. I have often wondered if after they retired, they wound up in jail somewhere. Such is the life of an air force scrounger. What a pair.

After the squadron was just about completely manned, I appointed one of the junior captains as theater officer and gave him all of the lieutenants, about six, as assistants. At 266 Tru Min Ky, where we lived in Saigon, there was a cover over the roof that made an excellent outdoor theater. The first thing they did was to set up a bar and hire Kim and Honey Bear, two very cute young Vietnamese women, as bar tenders. They served beer and Cokes and would mix a drink if you furnished the liquor. Most people brought their mixed drinks with them because if you gave the bartenders a bottle, your "friends" would make short work of it. Everyone had to bring their own chair. They got a projector from special services and had a new movie every night. Each night they started the movies with an XXXXX-rated movie. I never knew where they got those movies nor ever wanted to know.

This worked fine for a while, but we had a bunch of young RF-4 fighter pilots living with us, "the peanut butter and jelly set." All of the older fighter pilots found another place to live and moved out, leaving a young major as "den mother." When these guys came back from flying over North Vietnam, they needed to unwind and were not ready for bed. They were up most of the night raising hell; no one could sleep. I would have to get their "den mother" to shut them up, which worked fine for a while, but they would soon be back at it. Finally, we wrote a letter to the Wing commander saying it was a flying safety hazard, and he moved them all out. In the air force, if you ever want something done, mention "flying safety hazard" and you get quick results. Unfortunately one night some tracers flew low over the theater, and Kim and Honey Bear quit. Attendance dropped after that.

One night there was a banging on my room door. It was one of the navigators. He was a sight you would not believe. He had on jungle boots, under pants, a purple satin smoking jacket, and a flight cap. He was carrying his .38 pistol and was wild-eyed. He said, "Colonel, come quick, they have caught a Viet Cong!" I followed him to the entrance of our building. The Nung guards (Chinese mercenaries) we had guarding the place had some poor Vietnamese fellow buck naked on the ground and were stomping him to death. I made them stop. He was a prisoner of war, unarmed, and to kill him would have been murder. I went outside the walls and stopped a Vietnamese military police (QC) Jeep and turned him over to them. They may have taken him around the corner and turned him loose for all I knew. It was a crazy war.

Another night I was awakened by a lot of shooting. I went up on the roof to take a look and could see what appeared to be a fire-fight among our aircraft. I called the squadron commander and the squadron security officer. We got dressed, took the Jeep, and drove onto the base. As we approached the flight-line, we were stopped by an air policeman, who told us we could not go on the flight-line because of a fire-fight. We told him they were our planes and we had to go.

When we got to our area, the fight was just about over, but there were several VC dead bodies lying around. Some of our mechanics were still running. The VC had tunneled from a cemetery outside the base under a double eight-foot chain-link fence surrounding the base. They had thrown tarpaulins over the concertina wire that lined each side of the runways, climbed over, and run toward our planes. The first time our maintenance people realized the VC were attacking, a mortar shell went off behind one of the planes in the dock. Since the mechanics were unarmed, they took off running to our personal equipment building, where the M-16 rifles and personal side arms were stored to be carried on combat missions. Unfortunately the building was locked and in the confusion in the dark, the airman in charge could not unlock the weapons, so everyone kept running. Our people were winded, but none were wounded.

We did not arm our mechanics because we were afraid one of them might get spooked some night and shoot one of our own people. We left our protection to the professionals. We had air police in sand-bag revetments spread throughout the area.

When we got to operations, the air policeman guarding the area came up to me and pointed to the personal equipment airman and said, "Colonel, you've got to do something with that nut. He jumped in my revetment and grabbed me by the shoulders yelling, 'Shoot him! Shoot him!' I couldn't aim, so I hit him with my gun butt."

If the VC had been professionals, they could have wiped us out, but they were not, and the air police did an excellent job. One of the VC soldiers had pulled the pin on a grenade and was about to drop it in an engine nacelle when an air policeman, the one with the nut, shot him. The VC soldier dropped the grenade and fell on top of it. It was quite a mess. When the VC soldiers withdrew, they ran down a taxi-way directly into two revetments with air policemen armed with M-60 machine guns. We counted sixty bodies in the area. The air police said there were five more captured and turned over to the QC. The American troops called the QC "White Mice" because they wore white uniforms. The QC said there were sixty-five VC soldiers in the raid; all were killed. I suspect those that were captured were shot. I could hear an occasional gun shot the rest of the morning.

Some of our planes received bullet and shrapnel holes, but maintenance had enough of them patched up so that we met our scheduled take-offs the next morning. If it had not been so deadly, it could have been funny, but there is nothing funny about seeing the dead bodies of young men, regardless of which army they were in.

At night when I got back to my quarters, I would have a constant stream of people coming to my door wanting to go over problems they were having and wanting my advice. It finally got to the point that if I wanted some time to myself, I would have to turn out my lights, close the shutters, and pretend to be asleep. I would use a flashlight under the covers to read or write letters.

One day I received a panic call from 7th Air Force Operations. I was to send all our available aircraft to Da Nang Air Base, located in the northeast corner of South Vietnam. The marines were in trouble near the DMZ and needed help. It was early in our deployment, so I only had five aircraft to send.

Before the aircraft left for Da Nang, I was short one pilot. At the same time I received a call from a pilot assigned to us, who had just arrived from the States by commercial air. I picked him up from the flight terminal and took him to a room in our quarters. I told him to unpack enough clothing for four or five days because I was going to have to send him to Da Nang. I had flown with him before and knew he could fly, so I sent him along as one of the more experienced pilots. He had been in Vietnam about two hours when he was in combat.

We located the North Vietnamese infantry working its way through the jungle to get behind the marines. Based on our information, a B-52 strike was made on the suspected area. Each B-52 carried ninety-six 750- or 500-pound conventional bombs. I did not go into the strike area but I read the marine commander's report who did. It was pretty gruesome with body parts hanging from trees, etc.

The marine commanding general later sent a colonel to my operations to find out what we did. I asked the colonel if he had a special intelligence (SI) clearance. When he said that he did not, I told him I could not give him any information without one. He responded by saying, "If I go back and tell a three-star general I couldn't get the information he requested, he'll have my ass, and he'll still get the information." I thought, the marines were one of us, so what the hell; I briefed him. After I briefed him, he went back and briefed the general, who recommended us for the Presidential Unit Citation.

I received a call from the housing officer at Da Nang, who complained that one of our officers had given him hell about the living conditions of the quarters and the latrine. I had to go to Da Nang to calm everyone down. The latrine was a large facility and it was filthy. The housing officer agreed, but he did not have enough help to keep it clean and he pointed to a sign that read, "IF YOU HAD 1,000 PEOPLE CRAP ON YOU EVERY DAY, YOU'D BE DIRTY TOO." I just turned around and walked away. What could I say?

One evening I received a call from 7th Air Force Operations directing me to prepare an aircraft and crew for immediate launch. I was told that someone would report to our operations to brief us on a top secret mission. When the individual arrived, he was an army linguist. French President Charles De Gaulle was in Phnom Penh, Cambodia, and was scheduled to depart that evening for Paris. Our mission was to fly to Phnom Penh, blacked out (without running lights). We were to follow his plane so the linguist could pick up any transmissions he might make to Paris by radio and forward the information back to Washington, so that they would know almost as soon as Paris what De Gaulle had to say. Of course we never received any feedback on the results of the flight. I feel sure that if Intelligence did hear anything, it was kept quiet because Washington would not want the French or anyone else to know we were spying on the president of France.

I received orders to mount a special mission for which I was to report to 7th Air Force Operations and Intelligence. I was briefed that they needed information about enemy communications along the Ho Chi Min Trail, which came down from North Vietnam through the Mu Gia Pass between North Vietnam and Laos. Supplies and equipment were transported by porters and trucks down the trail to Cambodia and Laos and then into South Vietnam. Enemy surface-to-air missiles were known to be in the area and there would be considerable risk involved. If we ran into trouble over Laos, we could try to recover and land in Thailand. We also were to try to make visual sightings of any movement of troops or supplies in the area.

Considering the risk involved, I asked for a volunteer crew. I would be the aircraft commander and one of our older pilots agreed to go with me. Because of the distance involved it was necessary to refuel at Da Nang going to and from the area. We flew at ten thousand feet because of the mountainous terrain and to remain above small arms fire. From the time we went into Laos until we reached Mu Gia Pass, the Ho Chi Min trail looked like the surface of the moon because of all the bombing by our F-4s and B-52s. We suspected they had moved their trail into the jungle west of the trail where there were still trees to cover their movements. We saw nothing, but we did pick up some radio communications. We knew they were there and reported our suspicions back to 7th Air Force. Some months later, after I returned to the States, one of our planes was hit by a missile in that area and all crew members were lost.

About sixty miles northwest of Tan Son Nhut there was a mountain

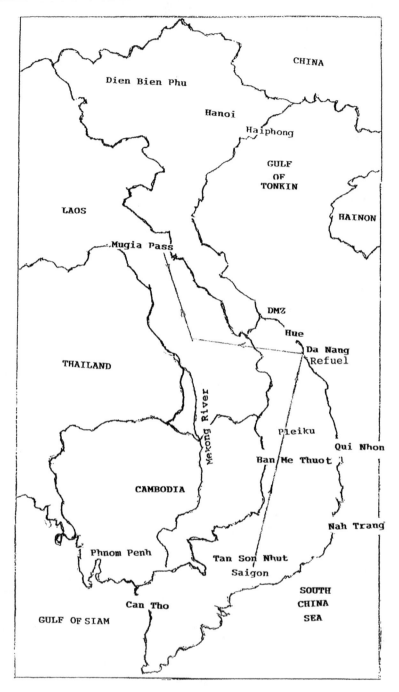

Author's sketch of his flight path on a special mission into Laos to collect information about enemy communications along the Ho Chi Min Trail.

named Mui Ba Din. It was cone-shaped and the sides were covered with jungle. The army had an observation and artillery fire base on top of the mountain. I was flying a mission in the area when we picked up two enemy radio signals about halfway up the north side of the mountain. I contacted the fire base and told them they had visitors and gave their location. They thanked me and told me to clear the area. In a few minutes the side of the mountain erupted with artillery fire from other fire bases in the area. The firing stopped and helicopters started bringing reinforcements into the fire base. I never found out the end result of the operation.

An inspection team from the Pentagon came to Vietnam to see how we were progressing and to see if there was anything we needed. A personal friend who served with me from the 308th Bomb Wing was on the team. I told him we were depending upon junior officers and young enlisted men to direct our missions and that SI clearances were essential for Jim and me.

Each week the army had a meeting at General Westmoreland's headquarters where missions were assigned for the coming week. After we had been in Vietnam about six weeks, Jim Jelley and I still had not received our top secret SI clearances. We had to rely on an ROTC first lieutenant to represent us. We would give him our capability and the sorties we could fly, and he would go to the meetings. When he came back, nothing matched our capability. I would give the poor lieutenant hell. He would say, "But, Colonel, they won't listen to me."

Jim's and my SI clearances finally arrived, so we decided to go with the lieutenant. When it became his turn to present our capability, the army colonel in charge completely ignored him. I got up and said, "I don't believe you heard what the Lieutenant told you" and he ignored me. Then Jim got up and said, "I don't believe you heard what the Colonel had to say, and until you are ready to cooperate, we aren't going to fly your goddam missions."

We got up and walked out and the young lieutenant was vindicated. When I got back to my office, I got a phone call from our deputy Wing commander. He said, "Al, what in hell did you guys do at that meeting?" I told him and he laughed and said, "This thing has gotten to the four-star general level, and they are about to have a fist fight."

Well, the army cooperated when forced to. It was the same attitude I ran into back at Geiger Army Air Field in 1946.

A close friend of mine, Army Lt. Col. Hobart Rowley, had been recalled to active duty and I got word that he was to arrive at Tan son Nhut. I met his plane and took him to the army personnel center on Tan Son Nhut. He was on orders to command an artillery battalion; however, when we reached the personnel center, he found that his orders had been changed and he was to stay at Tan Son Nhut as a member of the inspector general's team. He was very disappointed. His quarters were on the edge of Tan Son Nhut and we visited often while we were there.

We joined the army Officers' Club, where we associated with Hobart's army friends. They had a colonel's dining room that was air conditioned and where there were table cloths and waiters and the food was excellent. We enjoyed our visits there.

I had a constant battle with 7th Air Force personnel office. When we were forming the three squadrons, I sent people where we needed them. I would get a call from a major in personnel looking for someone and I would tell him where I sent him. He would get all excited and say, "You can't do that. He was on orders some place else." I would tell him I sent him where I needed him and to change the orders. To the major, I was a real son-of-a-bitch. So what? I was not in a personality contest.

While the city of Saigon may not sound like a war zone, it was indeed. One main problem was identifying the enemy. It was like trying to distinguish Republicans from Democrats. We received ground fire almost every mission; however, it was very inaccurate. We occasionally received battle damage, but it was never bad enough to abort a mission. One of the aircraft from another unit picked up twelve bullet holes before they got the landing gear up on takeoff from Tan Son Nhut. One of the squadron pilots came into my office carrying a leather cushion from a pilots seat.

He said, "I want to show you something." He pointed to a bullet hole in the back of the cushion. The bullet had come through the floor of his plane, a bulkhead, and the back of his seat before stopping in the thin padding next to his back. He did not think too much of my humor when I told him it was a shame that piece of leather cheated him out of a Purple Heart.

Another time a very upset navigator came into operations with a broken set of eye glasses. It seems he was looking through his drift meter when a bullet came up through the drift meter, breaking his glasses that he was wearing at the time.

One evening while I was landing at Tan Son Nhut, I picked up tracers from automatic weapons fire on the final approach at six miles and again at three miles out. Fortunately I did not get hit. I reported the incident to the control tower and infantry was sent out and the VC were all killed.

When this was brought up at briefing, the crews said the VC had been shooting at them for about a week, but they were lousy shots. Now that I had them killed, the VC might send out some good shots.

I found out that psychological warfare C-47s dropping leaflets over the jungle were seldom fired on. I contacted their headquarters at Tan Son Nhut and asked if I could have some of the leaflets. My idea was to try to disguise our mission. In a couple of hours a big truck pulled up to operations loaded with leaflets. I did not expect so many, but I accepted them and put a box of them on each aircraft. The flight engineer was to dispense the leaflets out the back door of the aircraft. I am not too sure they stopped the ground fire, but it became a requirement for all TEWS aircraft. I happened to overhear a couple of flight engineers talking. One of them said: "He's got us throwing out these damn leaflets and sure as hell, after the war, they'll make us pick them up."

I feel fortunate in that only one 361st TEWS aircraft was shot down. They flew too close to a mountain and the VC fired down on them. There were nine men on board and none survived. The VC got to the crash site first. Leaflets were strewn all over the area and all of the classified documents were mixed in with them. The VC soldiers did not recognize them for what they were. That could have compromised our mission. Instead they took boots, watches, wallets, personal articles, and weapons, but none of the electronic equipment or classified documents on board. For some strange reason, they cut off the tail wheel and took it with them.

An infantry platoon was air-lifted into the crash site to secure it from the enemy, so that the recovery team could remove the bodies of the flight crew. Because of the remoteness of the crash site, and knowing that the enemy was in the area, they did not attempt to secure anything from the aircraft. They placed thermite grenades on the wings and on all classified equipment completely destroying the aircraft.

Unfortunately the flight crews did not receive the feedback of the importance of the ARDF missions. This was mainly due to the classification of the project and the possibility that information might have been compromised to the enemy. Only the squadron commanders and operations officers of the EC-47 squadrons flying with top-secret SI clearances were allowed to land at either Tan Son Nhut, Nah Trang, Pleiku, or Da Nang and even they received very little feedback. I found out from friends in the Pentagon that the results of our missions were briefed each day by top air force officers. The flight crews never knew how the information we gathered was ever used. Based on the reports of the results of our support of the marines near the DMZ, we suspected a great many B-52 arc lights' strikes were based on the information we gathered.

Our units had top priority for supplies and equipment over any other units in Vietnam. For example, I received a frag order to send one of our aircraft on an extended sortie. To complete the mission, it was necessary to refuel at Plieku. I received a call from the aircraft commander saying the Plieku base commander refused to give him any fuel. I asked him if he explained that he was on a mission ordered by 7th Air Force. He said he had, but the base commander told him that fuel was precious and that he would not give any to a "Gooney Bird." With that I told the aircraft commander to return to Tan Son Nhut. In a couple of hours, I received a call from 7th Air Force operations wanting to know who in hell had ordered that sortie back to Tan Son Nhut. I told him I did. When he asked why, I told him. In a few minutes I got a call from a very meek Plieku base commander apologizing and he told me I could send any of our planes to Plieku and if the crews had any trouble, they were to contact him personally.

In the fall of 1966, I was flying as a replacement aircraft commander. We were assigned an area northwest of Tay Ninh called the Iron Triangle. During the six hours we spent in the area, we gathered a record of twenty-nine ARDF fixes. This obviously meant that there was a large enemy force in the area. After the data was reported to Intelligence, the area was saturated with artillery fire and air strikes. This was the beginning of the battle of Toledo. After the battle was over, fifteen hundred enemy bodies were counted. We later learned that division commanders and senior intelligence officers stated that without our ARDF findings, they would have been completely in the dark about the location of the enemy and their situation and tactics.

The 173rd Airborne Brigade made us a present of an artillery shell case that had been engraved thanking us for our support of their mission. At the time we thought it was very nice of them, but we never knew exactly why they were so grateful.

One day while I was flying northeast of Saigon, I heard air rescue trying to find a pilot in the jungle who had been shot down. The pilot had a portable radio and was trying to direct rescuers to his position without much luck. With the equipment I had on board, we were able to locate him. A1E fighters (Sandies) strafed the jungle around him to keep the VC away from him while he was being recovered by helicopters. After I located him, I continued with my regular mission.

I had two intelligence officers on my staff, a lieutenant colonel and a captain. I insisted that the crews going into a combat environment be given all of the current enemy capability at pre-takeoff briefings. The captain was the usual briefing officer.

His standard briefing was "Them Viet Cong is highly mobile. Y'all be careful, hear?"

It got to be a joke among some of the flight engineers. They made fun of him and mimicked him. I had warned both the captain and his boss, a lieutenant colonel, that their performance was unsatisfactory.

During the pre-takeoff briefing after I helped get the pilot out of the jungle, I asked the captain what happened that day. When he said, "No one got shot down." That did it. I told him to come to my office after the briefing where I relieved both intelligence officers. I then went to Wing headquarters to see the Wing intelligence officer. He told me he did not have a replacement other than two young ROTC second lieutenants. I told him I would swap a lieutenant colonel and a captain for the two lieutenants. They worked out fine. I told them exactly what I wanted and the crews had the latest intelligence at every briefing.

The American kids drafted off the campuses were not stupid, and it did not take long for them to figure out how ridiculous some of their orders were. For example, I was working in an area about forty miles north of Tan Son Nhut near An Loc and Loc Ninh, where the last battle of the Vietnam War was fought, when I came upon a road block. VC soldiers were collecting taxes from the Vietnamese farmers who were bringing produce into Saigon. I called Paris Control, whose duty it was to monitor the aircraft in the Saigon area, and asked them to send some fighters to knock it over. In a few minutes four AlE fighters showed up, but when their leader checked in with me, he told me we were in a no-fire zone and he could only fire in self-defense. I told him I would try to draw their fire. When I went back to the road block, the VC soldiers waved at me. They knew our rules of engagement.

About two weeks later I was back in the same area and the road block was still there. When I reported to Paris Control, I was told to forget it. They could not get the province chief's permission to fire on the VC. I could not believe it. We had to get permission from the enemy to attack their troops. You can be assured the military did not come up with that policy. Although some province chiefs were sympathetic with the VC, some were not, but were so afraid they or their families would be killed, they felt they had to cooperate with the VC or face the consequences.

On Christmas Day, 1966, I was ordered to mount two sorties, one along the coast around central South Vietnam and one in the central highlands. This was during a Christmas truce. I took the sortie in the highlands. I saw hundreds of trucks and carts bringing supplies south. The sortie on the coast reported hundreds of boats of all types also bringing in supplies. To me it is unbelievable that the enemy would be given an uninterrupted period for troop movements and resupplying their troops for an extended period or until the next truce. We had to comply with the truce; the VC did not. I feel certain that whoever ordered the truce would not have to face the re-armed, reinforced enemy and they showed little regard for the young troops who did. It could not be blamed on the military. It came directly from the "military geniuses" in the White House and the Secretary of Defense. It was politically motivated and it did not work.

At the beginning of my tour in Vietnam I had trouble getting awards and decorations for my crews. Because of the top secret classification of our operation, I could not state the reasons for the decorations. As a result my requests were disapproved. I finally appointed one of the majors in the squadron as awards and decorations officer. He and I went to the 7th Air Force awards and decorations office and finally convinced the right people that because of classifications, we could not give the exact reason for our requests, but when the major gave them a request, it should be approved.

One Sunday morning before church I went to squadron operations to check on what was going on, when I got a call from our maintenance officer that they needed to test-fly one of our aircraft. The test flight would not take very long so instead of calling the duty crew from the barracks, I decided the supervisor of flying, who was a pilot and was already on duty, and I would take the flight.

Shortly after takeoff I noticed an ox-driven cart piled high with straw on a road. Out of the side of the cart came perfect smoke rings and a lot of people were gathered around the cart. Every time I circled the cart, the people started moving away from it. Things did not seem right, so I called the Paris Control for a forward air controller. One happened to be in the area. He took one look and said that they were VC and for me to clear the area. In just a few minutes the area was blanketed by artillery fire. I have no idea how many people we killed. I went back to Tan Son Nhut, landed, and went to church. Ironic, isn't it?

One day one of the aircraft commanders came in my office and told me he had let his pilot land the aircraft, but he had lost control and that he (the air commander [AC]) had to take control to prevent an accident. I told him to send the pilot in, that I wanted to talk to him. When he came in, I could tell he was shaky and scared. I am sure he thought he was going to be grounded.

I told him, "I guess you expect to get your ass chewed. Well, you're not. I understand your problem. I know that you were a Navigator and have just recently graduated from pilot training. However, I'm not going to let you tear up one of our airplanes." I told him I wanted him to get twenty-five supervised landings and to get with the scheduling officer and make arrangements to fly with an instructor pilot. I told him that when he got his twenty-five landings to let me know and he and I would take a mission together.

When he got his landings, he reported back to me. I told him that he was going to fly as AC and I would fly as his pilot and that I would not do anything that he did not tell me to do. Everything worked great. I did not touch the airplane. At one point, however, some tracers went whizzing by and he gasped. "What's that?" I took control of the aircraft and took evasive action.

I told him when he rotated back to the States, he should apply for an assignment with the Training Command as an instructor pilot. The last I heard, he was a flight instructor and doing well.

I felt so sorry for the young infantry combat soldiers, especially those who were alone at night down in the jungle. Periodically tanks rumbled by our quarters heading for a battle, normally in an area northwest of Saigon. Each tank had one or two young men riding on top. They were fresh and clear-eyed in their clean fatigue uniforms. Ten days to two weeks later they would return showing the signs of battle. Men and tanks were covered with mud and you could see desperation in their eyes. God only knows what sights they had seen. They were not boys any longer, but battle-weary men.

In the evenings when I worked over a battle area telling the ground forces where the enemy was located and talking by radio to some soldier on the ground telling him that I had to return for more fuel, they would beg me not to leave them. It was hard for me to do. I had four sons their age or younger.

In December, 1966, I had some very severe chest pains. We had a young doctor attached to the unit who thought my problem was from long hours and pressure. He wanted me to go to the hospital for a few day's rest and observation. I turned him down but finally it got so bad I had to accept.

I was the only patient in a ward. I was given a shot that put me out for several hours. After I was awake for a short time, I got another shot. This went on for a couple of days. When I finally woke up the ward was full of very severely wounded soldiers. They were just teenagers, just babies. Some were crying for their mamas. There had been a big battle in Tay Ninh about sixty miles northwest of Saigon. The 3rd Army Field Hospital was completely full, so the overflow was being sent to the Tan Son Nhut Hospital. The boy in the bed next to mine was from Hawaii and was badly burned. The one across the aisle had been hit with three machine-gun bullets across his chest. The rest of the boys had various wounds and most were heavily sedated. Some were crying in pain.

In the corner bed there was a large black kid whose body was in a cast from his ankles to his waist, his right arm in a cast and a sling. The sling was covered with blood and a Purple Heart was pinned to it. His head and eyes were covered by a bloody bandage. I could tell he was from the South by his accent. He was crying for his mama. He had just about given his all for his country. I thought about the integration battles going on back in the States. If they could only have seen this young lad, they would have felt differently. I still break up every time I think of those wonderful boys. I pray that they all survived.

My chest pains were gone when I looked at those boys. I felt like a malingerer. I couldn't take it. I called the nurse and told her to get my clothes and that I was returning to duty. She said a doctor would have to release me. I know she was only following orders, but I am afraid I had to get a little rough with her verbally. She got my clothes, but I cleared her with the doctor later.

I went back to duty for only a short time and the pains came back. The doctor decided that I should be evacuated to the Air Force General Hospital at Tachikowa, Japan. I entered the hospital just as the new year 1967 was being celebrated. Talk about being lonely. The hospital was a relief though. The bed was nice and soft. I could take as many hot showers as I wanted and did not have to dive for the cover every time there was a loud noise. I was in the hospital about a week and had all kinds of tests. The pains were gone, so I took about three days to do some sight-seeing in Tokyo.

I reported back to the hospital and was told I was being evacuated back to the States. I told the doctor, "No, I am going back to Vietnam." I was very determined about going back, so he sent me to see another doctor. I told him I was going back to Vietnam because I was needed. I had built the squadron operations from the ground up and it was not ready yet to be turned over to someone who was not completely ready to assume command. He agreed to my insistence to return to Tan Son Nhut. As it turned out the last doctor was a psychiatrist. I guess they thought anyone who preferred to go to Vietnam over going home must be a nut. I am not too sure they were not right, but I went back to Vietnam. It was not entirely unselfish. If I did not complete my tour, I might have to return.

The air force had set up a program for the officers and men that they called "Rest and Recuperation (R&R)." The purpose of this program was to keep up the morale of the troops. Once during a tour of duty in Vietnam, they were allowed to take an R&R to any number of places in Asia away from the war. Pan American Airlines had some prop-driven aircraft that were no longer in use for regular passenger service. These were used to fly troops to R&R locations at no cost to the troops or the government. On these flights they provided the best of meals including first class steaks. To take advantage of this, I set up a program for our squadron for our troops to go as often as they wanted provided we did not sacrifice our mission.

The air force had an Allied Officers' School at Maxwell Air Force Base where officers from friendly nations could send their flight crews to the United States for training at our air force facilities. These officers were sponsored by U.S. officers when they were at Maxwell Air Force Base to help them with any problems they might encounter in a foreign land. During one class I sponsored captains from the Philippines, Finland, and Thailand. When I went to Bangkok, Thailand, for R&R, I met Major Nimol, who was one of the officers I had sponsored at Maxwell. He and his wife took me on a tour of Bangkok that the usual tourist would never have the opportunity to see. When we were in Montgomery, we took the officers we sponsored to our church. We were all in uniform and the church had a special greeting for them. So when I was in Bangkok, Major Nimol took me to a Buddhist temple. We were required to take our shoes off at the door and when we were inside, we sat cross-legged on the floor. The Thais are very short people. So there I sat a head taller than all the rest. I did not understand a word of the language, of course, so I just followed along the best I could.

One morning while I was in Bangkok, I was relaxing by the hotel pool enjoying life when a Thai civilian joined me and after we talked for a while, he invited me to lunch. I was suspicious wondering what he was up to, but he was so nice, I accepted. We went to a beautiful Chinese restaurant and had a multi-course dinner that lasted for more than two hours. When we finished, he drove me back to the hotel. I was stuffed. About an hour later Major Nimol and his wife picked me up to take me to dinner. We went to a Thai restaurant. Part of the meal included a very spicy bird's egg soup considered by the Thais to be a great delicacy. As full as I was, I managed to eat a bowl of it and when I finished, Mrs. Nimol, being a gracious hostess, refilled my bowl. I did not want to be rude, so I ate it, but I was really miserable.

Thailand is famous for its precious gems. I wanted to take something home for Eva, so Major Nimol took me to a gem dealer. The prices were marked on the gems, but with a word from Major Nimol, the prices dropped drastically. I purchased a necklace set with black sapphires with earrings to match.

At that time Thailand was a military-controlled monarchy. Major Nimol took me to meet his father-in-law, who was a lieutenant general in charge of all personnel in the Thai military services. He lived in a lovely home, was very gracious, and spoke very good English. His daughter, Nimol's wife, was educated at the Sorbonne in Paris. The Nimols are a very lovely family.

The military took over all the hotels in Saigon to house officers or NCOs except the Caravelle Hotel, which was left for the press and visiting VIPs. We enjoyed going to the bar in the Caravelle because it was quiet and it was on the top floor of the hotel where we could watch the war at night. After we had been there a short while, the waitress would bring a round of drinks, compliments of some man at the bar. He would then come by and join us. He would be a reporter looking for a story. We never told them anything of value and mainly just kidded them along. Even though we were in civilian clothes, I am sure they added to the story to their advantage and quoted us as "high military spokesmen." There were many stories about the war posted by the reporters who never left the Caravelle Hotel. I was not a great fan of the press corps because they downgraded the military and our mission. After all men were getting killed who were dedicated to their jobs. Much of the time these "high military spokesmen" were some young enlisted man who thought he knew more than his commander. Jim G. Lucas, one of the older war correspondents for *U.S. News and World Report*, refers in his book, *Dateline: Vietnam*, to the restaurant atop the Caravelle Hotel in Saigon as a meeting place for war correspondents.

I could go on for hours telling how the press reported what they wanted the American people to hear. Whether the information was correct or the source was reliable had no bearing on their reports. Some of the reporters could be very arrogant.

One day two of them showed up at our operations. They did not ask me if they could fly; they told me they were going to fly on one of my aircraft. When I told them no, they went into their standard "freedom of the press and the American people have a right to know" routine. I told them our mission was classified and we had classified equipment on board and that no big mouth was going to tell the American people AND the VC army what we were doing. I told them if they could get permission from 7th Air Force headquarters, I would let them fly. I knew they could never get permission. Then I told them these aircraft were going where there was a lot of shooting, and if they got permission, I hoped they got shot. They left with a lot of ill will toward me. I guess that worked both ways. I am sure I would not have reacted the way I did if the reporters had not been so arrogant about their intentions to fly in one of our aircraft.

The pilot on one of our new flight crews had been a public relations officer (PRO) in the Pentagon. He gave briefings to the press and ranking staff members. As a result he was well known, and when it became known by General Westmoreland's staff that he was in Vietnam, he was transferred to his staff. He lived in the room next to mine and when he was transferred, he asked my permission to keep his room. We became good friends. If his lights were on when I came home in the evening, I would stop and have a drink with him. He told me he could not understand the press reporters. They did not react to his briefings the way they had when he briefed them in the Pentagon.

Every evening at five o'clock, the reporters were briefed on the latest activities. He had been told to give the reporters all of the information available that did not compromise future operations, and above all, not to lie to them because if caught in a lie, it would completely discredit the military to the press. He said that when he briefed them on some incident that he knew was correct, the reporters would laugh and jeer, then one would call out and say, "Now this is what really happened" and proceed to give his version of what he thought happened. In most cases the reporter's version discredited the military. He said he knew the reporter's version was incorrect but there was no way he could convince anyone that it was wrong because the reporter claimed his version came from "a high military spokesman" or what he claimed he personally saw. The reporters' version was the one the American people saw on the evening TV news.

These briefings became known by the press as the "Five O'clock Follies." It is difficult to understand why the press reacted that way. I feel much of it was self-serving on the part of the reporters trying to make a name for themselves or bucking for a promotion. They seemed convinced that the military was trying to cover up something that they did not want people to know about, which was ridiculous. No doubt there were screwups during the war, but there is in any war.

The press played a very active role in shaping the opinions of the American people, especially the young people of draft age. This was the first time the horrors of war were televised and shown to the American people in their own living rooms. The reaction was mixed causing great differences of opinion among the people. There were some very dedicated members of the press corps who went to great extent to be objective about the Vietnam War. Some tried to find answers to the same questions I had about our involvement in the war.

The American people deserve to know the truth about what is going on during a war. They are understandably anxious when they have loved ones involved. With today's modern communications and people watching the war on television, it becomes difficult to keep people informed without endangering the lives of those in combat. The situation calls for responsibility, both on the part of the military and the press.

We had been in Vietnam about eleven months when an inspector from the Corps of Engineers inspected our quarters at 266 Tru Min Ky and condemned them. They claimed that they were about to fall down. The Vietnamese builder had not put enough concrete with the sand and the sand was washing away. We had to move immediately. We were given much better quarters. Most of the rooms were off of inside halls so there was not the concern for snipers. The rooms were larger, a little better furnished, and had a hot water heater that took the chill from the shower water. The squadron commander had returned to the States by then and I would have rotated too if it had not been for the hard time I gave 7th Air Force personnel. I roomed with a lieutenant colonel from Ft. Worth, whom I had taken aeronautical engineering with at Texas A&M.

About the same time the new Wing commander told me my replacement had arrived and was ready to take over my job. I could go home if I wanted to, but would have to have approval of 7th Air Force personnel. I put in a request. It came back disapproved and since I was surplus to the Wing, I was assigned to an AC-47 gun-bird outfit some place up-country. The major in personnel was getting his revenge. I ignored the orders to the gun-bird outfit, but had to stay in Tan Son Nhut another month. It was worth it. I had gotten the operations set up and the squadrons built without any interference from the major.

I received the Bronze Star for developing our operation and the Distinguished Flying Cross for discovering a large group of VC gathering to attack U.S. installations. After artillery fire and F-100s bombed the area, there was a body count of approximately fifteen hundred. It was the beginning of the Battle of Toledo.

All of the people who went to Vietnam about the time I did had orders back to the States and had already gone home. I was really sweating it out. Sergeant Layman, our first sergeant, brought me a wire with orders assigning me to Mountain Home Air Force Base, in Idaho as a backseat observer. After I got over the initial shock, I suspected some hanky-panky. It was not until I read the message several times, I found there was an error. My good friend, Sergeant Layman had gone to the 6994th Security Squadron to use their Teletype machine to send the fake orders. I would have been more gullible if I had not played the same joke myself on a fellow back in the 308th Bomb Wing at Hunter.

I was determined to return to Maxwell because my home and family were there and I wanted to return there. I used the commanders' communication network to call the personnel center at Randolph Air Force Base and told them what I wanted. They told me there was an opening for the base operations officer which was fine and I told them I would take it. They called me back and said it was taken, but they had an opening as inspector general of the Civil Air Patrol headquarters. I did not want the job but it was the only thing open at Maxwell.

At Tan Son Nhut small wooden boxes containing rat poison were placed throughout the base to control the rats. They were painted bright red and had the words RAT POISON printed on them in large black letters. They were open on each end and rat poison was placed inside. During the year when things would get rough, I would go behind the office and sit on a rat-poison box to take a breather. I did not think anyone noticed. Just before I left, the unit gave a going-away party for me. As a gift they presented me with a rat-poison box that they had upholstered. It is one of my favorite keep-sakes.

When I received my orders for Vietnam, I tried everything I could think of to get out of going. I knew the basics of Operation Phyllis Ann, but what I did not know was the end result of the operation. After I got to Vietnam, I found what I thought was the best job in Vietnam. I loved the comradeship and working with men on a project that was vital to the war effort. During my tour in Vietnam we received two Presidential Unit Citations and a third one after I returned to the States. When I boarded the plane for my return flight back to the States, I felt that I could look back and say "a job well done."

When it finally became my turn to return to the States, I could not find my shot record, so it was either take all my shots over again or stay in Vietnam. The Tine test was positive, which meant at some time I had been exposed or had tuberculosis. Every time I took a Tine test since I was in junior high school, the same thing happened. In the air force the results had never been questioned, until this time.

When we landed in Fairbanks, Alaska, on the way home, I was met by representatives of the federal health service who had been warned that I was coming. They treated me like Typhoid Mary and for a while, I did not think they were going to let me back into this country. I tried to tell them about my recurring problem with the Tine test, but they were not interested. They wanted me to check into the hospital at Elmendorf Air Force Base for observation and tests. I finally told them, "I am not going to the goddam hospital. I am going back to my family in Montgomery, Alabama." To keep them happy so I could continue on my way back to Maxwell, I had to agree to take a chest X-ray every month for a year and then every quarter for another year. What a waste of time, effort, and government money. They were just following orders like the rest of us, but I was not going to delay getting home for what I considered a frivolous reason.

I flew into Travis Air Force Base, California, on a civilian airline on contract by the air force. There was no welcome home. It was just a matter of getting on another civilian plane and flying to Montgomery, Alabama, where I was met by Eva and the boys. At least I did not get spit on as some of the returnees did.

When I went to Vietnam I was assigned a duty where I could use the knowledge I had gathered during twenty-five years of continuous military service. Considering the reputation, awards, and decorations the 360th TEWS received, we must have done a good job. I certainly cannot claim all the credit. Our maintenance personnel were outstanding considering the age of the aircraft. I cannot praise them enough. Our flight crews were real professionals as were our administrative personnel. All I had to do was provide operational leadership, direction, and purpose.

While in Vietnam I saw many things happen that were difficult for any professional military man to understand. It has become known that it was a war led by politicians in Washington who had absolutely no military experience and considered themselves superior to the Chiefs of Staff. I will leave it to the historians to evaluate the Vietnam War. Much has been written about the political aspects by those more qualified than I. I can only tell what I saw and experienced.

Five years after I returned from Vietnam, my son, Bob, went to Vietnam in the First Cavalry Division as a helicopter pilot. Any war that lasts that long without any hope of victory is unacceptable especially when it cost the lives of so many young men. The Vietnam experience will forever affect the way the American people will be willing to tolerate future military actions.

chapter 12

The Final Air Force Days

WHEN I ROTATED BACK TO THE STATES in June, 1967, I wanted to go back to Maxwell Air Force Base. We had bought a house in Montgomery and I had left Eva and the kids there. I had friends in the right places, so I was able to kill assignments to Special Air Warfare Branch of the Tactical Air Command, which would have been more of what I was doing in Vietnam, and would have required extended visits to Vietnam. I also had assignments killed to the Pentagon and to the headquarters of the Continental Air Command. Career-wise, this was a terrible mistake. Had I taken any of these assignments, I feel I could have advanced my career.

I took an assignment to the air force headquarters of the Civil Air Patrol (CAP-USAF) as the inspector general at Maxwell Air Force Base, Montgomery, Alabama, because it was the only opening available at Maxwell Air Force Base.

The CAP is a civilian auxiliary of the air force with the primary responsibility of search and rescue within the United States and endeavors to instill in young people the desire to fly. At the time I was involved, the air force loaned small surplus aircraft that were no longer in the inventory to the CAP for searching for missing aircraft and lost persons in remote areas. Private members also used their personal planes for searches. The air force paid for the fuel used during search missions.

Each state has a Wing headquarters and squadrons at various civilian airports within each state. As an air force auxiliary they have access to all military surplus material except weapons. CAP members wear air force uniforms and rank except for hat and lapel ornaments.

I was in charge of a team of inspectors who traveled around the country inspecting state Wings for search capability and compliance with air force directives. My inspection team consisted of one lieutenant colonel as director of inspection and three master sergeants who were specialists in supply, maintenance, and operations.

It was my duty as inspector general to determine the effectiveness of each unit and make recommendations to the air force and to the CAP commanders of the units. There are some very fine people involved in the CAP. They are very dedicated and give of their time and talents in working with young boys and girls to instill in them a desire to fly. One of the best units I inspected was the one in Oklahoma City. A squadron commander was a policeman who did an outstanding job working with young people. The California Wing was outstanding in complying with the CAP directives. However there were also some Wings whose people used the CAP to further their own agendas.

Prior to an inspection, I would send a letter to the Wing commander advising him of the date of the inspection. I wanted to determine the effectiveness of the organization and our inspection team could not be as effective in a social environment. They are supposed to instill a desire for flying in young people, which hopefully they do. However, at that time they took advantage of their situation to raise money that was spent on lavish parties for a small group of top commanders and their wives.

I discovered some of the civilians in charge of the CAP were very powerful politically. Although it was an air force auxiliary, CAP-USAF headquarters had very little control over the CAP. For example, a former CAP supporter, who was a millionaire friend and financial supporter of President Johnson, got CAP-USAF headquarters moved from Ellington Air Force Base near Houston into a new building that had been designated for the ROTC headquarters at Maxwell Air Force Base. When the air force commander of CAP-USAF tried to gain control of the CAP, the previously mentioned CAP commander called President Johnson and told him there was a "dead general" there, and asked him to please remove the "body."

Another CAP commander, who was a multi-millionaire from Delaware, wanted the CAP rank of the commander to be increased to brigadier general. Fortunately the air force held the line and refused his request. Some, but not all, CAP officers liked to try to pass themselves off as real air force officers.

Two regional commanders had a regulation passed that all CAP members must have insurance for injuries suffered while on CAP duty, which is fine. However, one of the regional commanders owned the insurance company and another one owned the bank where the money was deposited that was collected from the members at an interest rate well below the going interest rate at the time. They were collecting ten dollars a year from each cadet in the United States. What a money-making deal and of course, the air force had no control over it.

During an inspection of one of the Wings, the supply inspector uncovered a discrepancy in supply records. There were records of thousands of high-value items, such as Jeeps, trucks, generators, radio equipment and radio stations, and various pieces of field equipment that could be used for camping, that could not be accounted for. There were no records as to where the items were located. When I confronted the Wing commander, a CAP colonel, he was very evasive. I told him I would stay indefinitely until I found all the government material. At that point he told me he knew where it was and we could take a flatbed truck and pick up the equipment, but in so doing, we would black out a lot of ranches in the area because they all had air force generators. We would also break up the communication systems because the ranches all had air force communication equipment. The trucks and Jeeps were also at these ranches. He told me he intended to contact the state senator, who at that time was very powerful in the U.S. Senate. He also stated he did not think the senator would be very happy with the air force in general and me in particular.

It finally came to me why the Wing commander, a CAP colonel who was an obscure air force reserve captain, had a mobilization assignment in Washington D.C. He was the senator's "number one boy" who was buying votes for the senator with misappropriated air force property. I contacted my commander and explained the situation to him. He asked me what my recommendations were. I recommended that the Wing be prevented from getting further access to surplus equipment, but the senator had too much power and I thought that I should probably take my inspection team on to the next inspection. The general agreed so I left with political thieves openly stealing from the air force.

The CAP-USAF director of materials came to my office with a list of identification numbers of the light aircraft on loan from the air force to the CAP Wings. He also had the FAA's list of aircraft owners and their aircraft listed by aircraft identification numbers. We crossed checked the two lists with a CAP member's roster. I was not surprised to find that more than half of the aircraft on loan were listed as being owned by CAP members—in other words stolen from the air force. The aircraft were no longer in the air force inventory and it had no use for them, but to me, it was the principal of stealing from our government. Had we taken appropriate action to recover them, it would probably destroy the CAP. Again CAP-USAF had no control.

One day I received a visit from an FBI agent. He told me that an army supply depot at Allentown, Pennsylvania, had donated about 100,000 pairs of army boots that did not meet army specifications to various government-sponsored organizations as well as the CAP. They were to be used only for the members of those organizations; however, the boots were beginning to show up in civilian shoe stores all along the east coast. The FBI agent wanted to be sure we did not interfere with their investigation. I do not know what the final results were.

Some of the people in these state units completely lose perspective. One day the commanding general of CAP-USAF called me into his office and told me to go out to one of the units and see the Wing commander. "Go out and find some reason to fire that son-of-a-bitch. He thinks he's General LeMay." I went into his office and found him sitting behind a great big desk in full uniform with flag stands behind him, smoking a big cigar. On the wall were pictures of the president, the governor, and General LeMay. I think he expected me to salute him when I walked in. Finding a reason to fire him was not hard to do. I encountered one unit whose members were in a pitched battle over canteens, mess kits, a broken film projector . . . just a bunch of junk.

When we went out to inspect the Hawaiian unit, the air force liaison officer told me that the CAP people had gotten their hands on a surplus provost marshall's staff car. It had the CAP shield on the side doors making it appear like an official vehicle. It had flashing red lights and a siren, and at night it appeared to be an emergency vehicle. The CAP people would gain access to the base by turning on the lights and siren as they approached the main gate at Hickam Air Force Base, and the air policeman on the gate would salute and wave the vehicle through thinking it was an air force officer.

I could not get binoculars for my crews in Vietnam, yet one of the Wings gave a very expensive pair of binoculars to anyone who would join the CAP. This was mostly an air force accounting problem but it shows how the CAP members were using their influence in high places to get their hands on government property. I was completely disgusted by the way some of these civilians cheated and stole from the air force. When I tried to enlist the aid of the FBI, I was told they had no jurisdiction because it was an air force auxiliary. When I tried to get help from the Air Force Office of Special Investigations (OSI), they said the CAP was a civilian organization and they had no jurisdiction. I was frustrated in every effort I made to gain some control.

A national convention was scheduled to be held in Los Angeles. The air force flew C-47s all over the country picking up CAP members to take them to the conventions at government expense. I flew down to Florida to pick up a group and as we were heading to Los Angeles, they asked me to land at Las Vegas. They had no intention of going to the convention. They were only taking advantage of the government's free transportation. I told them my orders were to take them to Los Angeles and that is where I was going to take them. They became angry with me because they were going to have to pay for their own transportation from Los Angeles to Las Vegas. They asked me if I would pick them up at Las Vegas for the return trip. I told them what time I was leaving Los Angeles and if they were not there, I would leave without them. They went to Las Vegas at their own expense and were back in Los Angeles for the return trip to their respective homes.

A few of the air force's senior officers who were involved and about to retire saw the CAP as a possible way of feathering their nests after retirement. They put themselves at the service of the more wealthy and influential members of the CAP. For example, after one of their lavish parties at Maxwell Air Force Base, two staff members from the Ohio Wing asked to be flown back home by air force transport. One of them wanted to get back in time to attend church services. The other one wanted to sleep late. The air force commander of CAP-USAF provided two aircraft for their convenience. I flew the second one and passed the first one on his way back. The temptation to play along with these millionaires and politically influential people is more than some people can handle.

In the September, 1999, issue of *Air Force* magazine, the following article appeared:

> Federal agents with search warrants seized Civil Air Patrol records, data, and computer files in five states on July 21. The FBI and the Air Force Office of Special Investigations confiscated records at the CAP national headquarters at Maxwell Air Force Base, Alabama, and at wings in Kentucky, Texas, Florida, and West Virginia in conjunction with "the alleged misuse of appropriated funds by CAP personnel," said AFOSI spokesman Major Steve Murray.
>
> The seizures were the latest development in a controversy that has gotten progressively worse since an Air Force audit in 1996 found significant problems in CAP financial management and accountability, flying safety, professionalism, and standards of conduct.
>
> The CAP is a civilian auxiliary of the Air Force and receives about $28.3 million in federal funds each year through the Air Force budget.

In May, the Senate Armed Services Committee sought a reorganization of the CAP, with a new board of directors to be appointed by the Secretary of the Air Force. An amendment to that bill postponed action until a year-long review of the matter was concluded.

According to Donna Leinwand of Gannett News Service, "The Air Force accused the 60,000 member group, known for its search and rescue operations, of mismanaging federal money, traveling first class on the taxpayer tab, retaliating against members who pointed out abuses, and losing track of its equipment. Auditors said they could not account for 70 percent of the federally purchased communications equipment in one branch of the group." Civil Air Patrol officials have denied the allegations.

The inspection and seizure of these records is long overdue. While there have undoubtedly been some changes in the operations and control of the CAP, the principle is still the same. Get all you can from the government.

Any time citizens write to their congressman or senator or to the executive branch, the letters are passed on to the Legislative Liaison Branch in the Pentagon and then to the inspector general of the unit involved. The unit then has seventy-two hours to answer. As the inspector general of the CAP-USAF it was my duty to reply to the letters. Most of the letters were petty complaints not worthy of investigation; however, they must have a reply. As an example I received a picture of a naked women laying on a round bed. The note with the picture said, "See how the men in the Air Force are ruining the morals of our people." My answer was, "I see no connection between the lady lying on the bed and the United States Air Force."

I received one letter stating that the writer had seen a woman in civilian clothes in an air force staff car. The note said, "Is this the way our tax money is being spent?" There was no time nor location given, which made it impossible to investigate. I replied that there are women in the United States Air Force and that with the little information given, I could offer no further comment.

After a couple of years of the inspector general fiasco, I had just about all I could take. I did not think they would ever consider me for the position of chief-of-staff, so when they started talking about another year in Vietnam, I felt my family needed me more than the air force needed me in Vietnam, so I retired. This was probably another career mistake, but I was ready to move on. So on August 1, 1969, I retired.

In general I loved the air force life; however, there were times when I wondered, "What in hell am I doing here?" But that is all part of air force life. I feel sorry for people whose occupations require them to do the same thing day in and day out. The requirements of the air force are strenuous, but I prefer that to a dull daily routine.

I love to fly but I was only able to accumulate more than eight thousand hours. The more rank you had, the less time you could spend in the cockpit. Because of my young age, I could have stayed in for another six years and I have always been sorry I did not take one of the assignments offered on my return from Vietnam, especially the one with Tactical Air Command.

I will always miss flying and even more the camaraderie of the troops. They are memories that will always be dear to me. One other thing that I have noticed since I retired is that I cannot always depend on what someone says. In the air force when an officer tells you something, you can always rely on his word being truthful.

After I retired, periodically, I received letters from the air force reminding me that I am still in the air force, only on the retired roll, and could be recalled at any time at the pleasure of the president, and that he did not need the approval of Congress. My reaction? "Don't throw me in that briar patch, Brer Fox."

At the 308th Bomb Wing reunion in August, 1996, in Omaha, Nebraska, we were given a tour of Offutt Air Force Base, which was where SAC headquarters was located. We conducted a memorial service at the base chapel for all of the men from the 308th Bomb Wing who are no longer living. As we entered the chapel, there was a listing of all of the people who were killed flying missions for SAC. I knew many of the names. On one wall of the chapel there are three stained-glass windows: one for the 2nd Air Force, the 8th Air Force, and the 15th Air Force. On the other wall there are stained-glass windows with the insignia for each of the Bomb Wings. It makes an old pilot feel good to know that someone remembers and cares about the sacrifices they made. There is a SAC museum near Offutt where examples of all the aircraft assigned to SAC are on display. They brought back many memories because I had flown many of them. For a while I felt I was back home as I do any time I am on an air force base. I guess I will always feel the air force is my home.

I look back on my life in the air force with pride, a feeling of accomplishment, and thankfulness that I was given the opportunity to serve, doing something I loved. As I look into the future and think of my great-grandchildren and their great-grandchildren, I hope they will read this and learn more about me as a real person and not just a name and date on a tombstone. I hope they will attempt to live their lives based on the code of a military officer: DUTY, HONOR, COUNTRY, AND FAITH IN GOD, because without His guidance, I would never have survived. He was with me all the way.

Index

Taihoku, Formosa (Taiwan), 36, 37, 43

Tan Son Nhut, Saigon, 143–73

Tarawa Island, 27, 28

Terrell, Cadet James, 14

Texas A&M University, 8–12, 71

38th Air Division, 111, 121

308th Bomb Wing, SAC, 103–29

308th Bomb Wing Command Post, 118–29

360th Tactical Electronic Warfare Squadron (TEWS), 144, 146

Tibbets, Col. Paul, 114, 118–20

Tsushima Straights, 31, 57

United States Air Foreces Europe (USAFE), 113, 124

U-2, 117

Vietnam, 140–70

Yangtze River, China, 31, 40–45

Zech, Lt. Donald, 27, 47

ISBN 1-58544-386-7